MOUNTAIN
TO
COAST

KELLY & STONE
ARCHITECTS

MOUNTAIN TO COAST

KELLY | STONE ARCHITECTS
20 HOUSES

Vladimir Belogolovsky
Foreword by Peter Morris Dixon

images
Publishing

Introduction

Vladimir Belogolovsky

Going through the arresting photos of the many gorgeous houses designed by Keith Kelly and Tim Stone, the founders of Kelly|Stone Architects, I am as fascinated by the enviable lifestyles of their occupants as by both historical and modern architectural precedents that may have inspired them. Their designs are surely underpinned by thoroughly researched exemplary architecture but most of all I feel privileged to peek into the lives of the owners of these extraordinary homes. These houses are admirable in their own right.

"Our mission is to design amazing homes in amazing places for amazing people. More than once, a client would say, 'Design something magnificent!'" exclaimed Stone when I discussed with the partners the design intentions behind their architecture. In this volume, the architects' work is represented by twenty houses handpicked from hundreds of their homes built mostly across North America over the last sixteen years. These structures transmit a sense of integrity, serenity, artistry, and domesticity. Persistently there is just the right balance between the traditional and modern. First and foremost, these houses are livable places beautifully inserted into distinct settings in close proximity to nature. They proudly reveal their soaring spaces, exposed structures, rich palette of natural materials, refined details, and, of course, masterfully framed sweeping views of scenic mountains and coastlines.

The book's focus on domestic architecture is hardly unconventional. After all, many of the leading architects are known primarily for their experimental houses. And it is precisely the free-standing, single-family house that has always served architects as the most fundamental, even essential, laboratory for architectural experimentation. What is quite remarkable here is that Kelly and Stone chose to build their practice entirely on unique luxury homes. This preoccupation has become their market niche. More so, the absolute majority of their houses are secondary vacation homes. In fact, only three of the houses featured in this album are primary residences. The rest are second homes. The architects started designing houses early on, since their apprenticeship time. Soon, they felt they were quite good at it. Both found freedom within this narrow focus—much more than in bigger commercial commissions, which are limited by such constraints as building codes, budgets, construction quality, impersonal management committees, and corporate boards.

Another important point that Kelly brought up in our conversation was that, "I like the kinds of relationships we are able to build with our clients. Some keep in touch even ten years later, asking us for advice about their houses. We cherish these relationships; they've become very personal."

It should be pointed out that the architects' houses are antitheoretical. Both partners admitted to me matter-of-factly that even at school they kept a safe distance away from architectural theory, focusing from the start on how to design buildings that work. Their houses represent a completely different breed of architecture from the uncompromisingly modern explorations of many of the seminal architects of the twentieth century. Such formal inventions as disciplined Corbusian white boxes, so-called "machines for living in" that slavishly tended to articulate the new architecture's five points rather than responding to the specificity of their site's topography and alluring views, and addressing the client's brief, so often dismissed outright on principle by many early modernists.

To better understand houses designed by Kelly and Stone, we need to free ourselves from such architectural precedents as the universal "less is more" prism-like houses by Mies, intellectual and contradictory exercises by Venturi, program-defying formal inventions by Koolhaas, or Eisenman's even more radical random juxtapositions. These were all important undertakings, but they are more about probing and testing their clients' ability to adapt to their architects' designs, not how they might enjoy comfort and tranquility to the fullest. In contrast, Kelly and Stone don't forget even for a moment that architecture directly affects the lives of those who will be living in their houses, therefore, there is no sacrifice of function for style. Yet, no one would shy away from asserting Kelly|Stone Architects-designed houses as stylish; they certainly are.

On the other hand, the partners are fully aware of the work of their colleagues. In that sense, one could say, they don't work alone. Three homes—Anglers Court, Radium Hot Springs, and Carson Vista—are influenced by the prairie-style houses of Frank Lloyd Wright. Other houses, at least in part, evoke the work of Greene and Greene's Arts and Crafts architecture. There is an evocation of Fay Jones' organically sensitive wood structures. And some of the houses in Hawaii, in particular, Hale 'o Luna O Ka Lāla, are inspired by the work of the mid-century modernist Vladimir Ossipoff. Of course, Kelly and Stone are also motivated by many contemporary masters, mostly those who work on a domestic scale in America and especially on the West Coast. Among those who should be mentioned are such celebrated firms as Olson Kundig, Walker Warner Architects, and Bohlin Cywinski Jackson. Nevertheless, these influences are quite subtle and in no way decisive. They are rather used as a depository of ideas, sensitivities, and techniques to be reexamined and engaged creatively to form the architects' own distinct design attitude.

The partners insist on designing houses for their clients, not for themselves. And it is true that every house in their portfolio is bespoke and responsive to the specific objectives of each client and site conditions. What is also true is that over the years, quite a few clients contacted Kelly and Stone to reflect on what they have achieved before, and that lineage helped to hone their techniques and skills, forming certain commonalities, even a recognizable visual language. Broadly defined as mountain-contemporary architecture, these structures can surely be identified as a family, metaphorically speaking. There is a strong continuity in their prevailing design strategies, features, and preference for particular materials that are carried from one project to the next.

Keith Kelly and Tim Stone founded their practice in 2006. Stone heads the company's original office in Steamboat Springs, Colorado, and Kelly manages their second office, which opened in Truckee, California in 2012. Kelly was born in 1970 in Tampa, Florida; his family moved a lot, living in Dallas, Kansas City, and throughout Colorado. He came into architecture simply by observing his father who worked a lot on improving family homes and fixing cars. The architect told me that he virtually grew up with tools in his hands. He took an architectural drafting class in high school and studied architecture at Texas Tech University. He then apprenticed in Dallas and Colorado.

Stone was born in 1974 in Aurora, an eastern suburb of Denver. He earned a bachelor's degree in environmental design from the University of Colorado Boulder and a Master of Architecture degree from the University of Colorado Denver. He has a hands-on approach to design, driven by his love for detailing and craftsmanship. Parallel to his architectural career, Stone has become a skilled welder, carpenter, photographer, and artist. Prior to co-founding their practice, the partners worked as project architects at Charles Cunniffe Architects. The practice, with a predominantly high-end residential portfolio, is headquartered in Aspen and operates several smaller locations in the mountains of Colorado. While working at the firm's Steamboat Springs office, chartered by Kelly,

the partners realized how well they could collaborate independently. It was that awareness that led to their daring move to start practicing on their own.

What makes the architects' houses particularly remarkable is that they are both familiar and surprising, even startling at times. There is a consistent strategy at play: break a single volume into a series of interconnected parts or pavilions that are then fragmented further into elements in terms of structure, décor, and cladding materials. There is always a strong commitment to building a layered complexity and multiplicity of characters. There is a sense of a journey and anticipation of transformative discoveries. These houses greet visitors with formality and sobriety. Come inside and the focus will be drawn to such features as a specially designed fireplace, kitchen stove, connecting stairs, or a vaulted ceiling propped up by sculpturally expressive trusses. Yet, these interiors are always dominated by the way the surrounding views are embellished and celebrated. And then there are backyards, typically eye-catching and integrated into the landscape with the architecture using every opportunity to blur the boundaries between inside and out.

This well-paced and choreographed design strategy is quite genuine to the architects whose work reflects their desire to connect to nature. Both grew up in houses and built similar homes for their own families, residing in small mountain communities, and enjoying outdoor lifestyles. In fact, Pearl Street, one of the houses featured in this book, is Tim Stone's current home. It was designed in two stages. First, a two-car garage on the rear side of a long rectangular lot with a two-bedroom dwelling unit above was done before his twin boys were born. It was later expanded when a much larger home was built at the front end of the property, which was almost entirely constructed by the architect himself. And now he is working on building another house for his family. This perpetual building, of course, is a constant stimulus for perfecting the ideal image of what constitutes a family home, both in how it is integrated with nature and in terms of designing memorable interiors peppered with strikingly beautiful features.

Many of the architects' distinctive findings are derived from their obsessive ways of working directly with such materials as exposed structural steel, timber framing, stone-clad accent walls, and extensive glazing. These integrate to bring a sense of balance, proportion, and refinement. Their buildings' most original characters, forms, and components are achieved when bold geometry and contrasting materials—rammed earth walls, exposed steel, natural stone cladding, timber framing, and wood-and-metal panels—are combined in ways that are exploratory and playful.

Carson Vista is among the architects' most daring structures. Its heroic posture is assembled out of improbably long and perfectly flat cantilevers extended over orthogonally stacked volumes with glazed corners that open in good weather and seemingly transform a building into pure abstraction. Hinman Creek is another expressive structure, a fan-shaped group of jointed orthogonal pavilions with extensive roof overhangs and massive, dynamically sculpted timber trusses and purlin extensions. The house is conceived as a hierarchy of hefty gable roofs, sheds, and canopies held in place by a variety of expressive trusses and columns.

There is a sense of fluidity in the architects' work. Ideas are tested, developed, and refined from project to project. As Stone pointed out, "All my best ideas flow from the tip of my pencil." There is an ongoing reinvention of what has already been achieved. One such unceasing line of exploration is the design of wood-and-steel trusses. They have become the design staple of Kelly and Stone houses. The partners often collaborate on their design and execution with Spearhead, a celebrated timber and steel fabricator out of Nelson, British Columbia, Canada. These overtly expressed structural members evoke kinetic sculptures accented by dramatic lighting.

The book introduces us to just a tiny fraction of the architects' total output, which numbers more than 400 houses, about two-thirds of which were built. In addition to California and Colorado where the architects have designed about 60 percent of their projects, 40 percent are in the Lake Tahoe area and 20 percent in Steamboat Springs. About 30 percent stand in Hawaii and the remaining 10 percent are in other states and various provinces of Canada. In recent years the practice generates about fifteen houses per year, after a period when it peaked at around forty active projects at any given time. The architects slowed down quite deliberately by focusing on larger projects, devoting more time and resources to designing each house as a work of art to be lived in.

Among the twenty houses in the book, nine are in California, five in Colorado, four in Hawaii, one in Nevada, and one in British Columbia. Curiously, a number of California houses are situated in Martis Camp, a private ski and golf resort with a luxury second-home community outside of Truckee, north of Lake Tahoe. This fact reveals another interesting detail about Kelly|Stone Architects' preoccupation, which is designing high-end houses in some of the most desirable residential communities. In addition to Martis Camp, the practice is active in the Muskoka lake region, about two hours north of Toronto, where several of their boathouses and cottages are now under construction. Another focus is on Koloa, Kauai, referred to as the "Garden Island" of the Hawaiian archipelago. These areas typically have great contractors and carpenters that make building very high-end houses possible. Once the architects discover such lucrative areas they tend to return again and again to build more houses there. Over the years, the partners noticed that many of their homes have influenced local communities. They told me that quite a few houses that are being built in these developments tend to emulate their work by exploring similar combinations of materials and more experimental geometry—going from mainly regional architecture to more contemporary.

Many of the houses in the book are quite large—between three and nine thousand square feet—and some push the cost upwards of $15 million. Without citing details that could reveal the identities of their owners, the book's descriptions all touch on the lives of those who call these envious places their homes. They are tech industry innovators, executives in pharmaceutical companies, bankers, lawyers, entrepreneurs, and business owners. For example, the clients for Fairway Overlook in Martis Camp are a retired couple from Las Vegas. They used to run a highly reputable entertainment business focusing on organizing private parties and corporate events with famous entertainers.

Kelly|Stone Architects employ twenty architects, split roughly in half between the two offices. Projects are often discussed and developed collectively, and their employees are regularly flown back and forth to cross-pollinate the design process, exchange skills, and immerse staff in local culture. Still, although there are a lot of conceptual and aesthetic crossovers, the partners lead their own projects, which results in visual distinctions between their houses. By and large Stone's work is more influenced by traditional and craft-oriented design. His houses are warmer and more eclectic. He underlines the importance of mass and proportion. We can tell which houses are designed by him: columns land on stone piers, there is an intuitive use of material, and heavy members support the light ones. Nothing is too slender. If the structure needs to be overdesigned to appeal to him visually then it needs to be overdesigned. "Anything that's worth doing is worth overdoing," Stone asserts with authority. "I am a bit of a purist; if there is a beam, it better be doing the work," he reassures me.

Kelly is a purist in his own right. He is pursuing a more abstract image of architecture. His houses are somewhat cooler, sleeker, and more rigorously stylized. They put on display more exposed concrete, metal panels, and glass as opposed to wood, natural stone, and reclaimed materials as preferred by Stone. He tends to employ orthogonal geometry, clean straight lines that accentuate flat horizontality. Yet, these discrepancies between the two architects are downplayed, and plenty more common features come through and often make their identities subtle, even confused. Thunderbird Court is the most

representative case in point. It combines features that are characteristic of both architects. Both principals like to highlight structural components, expose, and express them; nothing is concealed. They strive to bring together various materials into a harmonious whole. Their houses lay into their sites eloquently while acknowledging regional qualities. They are the kind of houses that one feels good to be in. They provide warmth and elevate the spirits of their residents. To Kelly, "An ideal house is a legacy home that people would pass from one generation to the next." All these qualities are reflected in the houses featured in this album and hundreds of others designed by Keith Kelly and Tim Stone, two very cool entrepreneurs who happen to be talented architects, whose work complements their awe-inspiring settings surrounded by mountains and along coastlines.

"Architecture should seamlessly integrate with its surroundings, respecting and drawing inspiration from the unique qualities of sites, landscapes, and climates. As designers, our commitment is to craft spaces that not only honor these contexts but also should elevate, inspire, and provide comfort. A home, in our vision, goes beyond shelter, serving as a harmonious extension that supports the lifestyle of its occupants while fostering a profound connection to the natural world."

- Keith Kelly, AIA, and Tim Stone, AIA

FAIRWAY OVERLOOK

Truckee, California, 2017

Situated on a steep hilltop wooded site, a fairly isolated location at Martis Camp ski and golf community of luxury private homes near Truckee, California, this mountain retreat stands out for its uncompromisingly modern character and arresting posture. The spacious six-bedroom house is masterfully shaped into three interconnected wings under the wide-angled geometry of butterfly roofs, a fitting image for the surrounding gently sloped mountains of the Carson Range and Pacific Crest, and the graceful wings of soaring solitary hawks. Fairway Overlook is unlike any other home designed by Keith Kelly, primarily due to its steel-frame structure, sleek minimalist spaces and surfaces, and the conspicuous absence of Kelly|Stone Architects' emblematic sculpturally expressive wood-and-steel trusses. Curiously, it is Kelly's favorite project, due to both its contemporary aesthetics and because of his fond memories of the amicable collaboration between the architect and his adventurous clients.

The house is home to a retired husband and wife couple from Las Vegas. They used to run a highly reputable entertainment business with a focus on organizing private parties and corporate events with famous entertainers. The architects were originally hired to remodel their existing house on Lake Tahoe, just 20 miles to the south from here. But as the work on that design proceeded it became apparent that both the house and its site had limitations. Martis Camp came into the picture quite naturally because over the years the architects have realized a number of their houses here. And it was Kelly who helped to select the appropriate lot.

Apart from extensive double-height clear glazing, which makes the house, at least when looking through its huge great room, largely transparent, the exterior walls are made of several contrasting materials. Low walls are mainly made of poured-in-place form-board concrete, while most other areas are clad in clear cedar, which extends to roof soffits and beams, and gray natural stacked stone that wraps around walls and chimneys. There are also metal panel accents; they are used extensively on walls, roof fascia, doors, windows, and columns. The gray stone, which came from Canada, was chosen to respond to the clients' request to introduce materials that were not common in this community before.

Most of the spaces here occupy the main level, a few steps below the formal square patio at the front and three-car garage to the side, a perpendicularly attached wing that also houses a two-bedroom suite upstairs. Besides back-of-house storage and a mechanical room, a wine cellar is the only fully furnished space in the basement. There is also a passenger elevator that links all three levels. The opposite side of the house overlooks expansive mountain views and a canyon toward the development's clubhouse. A large terrace with an oversized gas firepit table with plenty of seating all around it is accessed through a huge, more than thirty-foot-wide wall that opens entirely with the help of six sliding pocket doors. The terrace steps down the slope to form a series of interconnected patios that are defined by board-formed concrete walls, and planters, and dotted with large boulders all along the adjacent wooded territory. Some of the same materials are carried from the exterior to the interior—walls of the gray stacked stone, clear cedar ceiling, accent areas finished in blacked metal panels along walls, floor fascia, and wrapped around structural elements. There are also wall accents made of polished concrete.

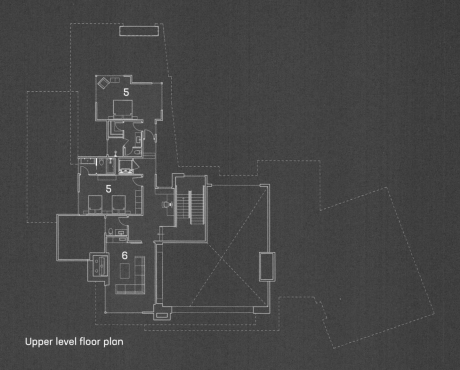

Upper level floor plan

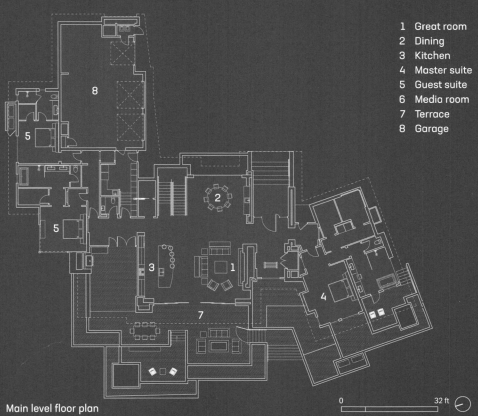

Main level floor plan

1 Great room
2 Dining
3 Kitchen
4 Master suite
5 Guest suite
6 Media room
7 Terrace
8 Garage

0   32 ft

The interiors in this house are primarily characterized by their huge sleek spaces with all key design features dramatically restrained and superbly crafted. The most striking part of the house is most certainly its centrally situated great room with a mezzanine gallery, all under a sloping ceiling that ranges from seventeen feet to twenty-one feet. This open and seemingly unbound space that incorporates a kitchen with a concealed butler's pantry and a roomy dining area is conceived as a club-like entertainment lounge. It is designed around a huge, full-height fireplace feature and an elegant stair in one of its corners.

The stair that connects all three levels commands its own attention. It was fabricated by Spearhead, an acclaimed Canadian company that specializes in the design and fabrication of architectural timber and steel. The artwork-like piece is distinguished by superb workmanship; all structural elements are prefabricated and welded together to hide any traces of assembly, while massive-looking white oak treads seem to magically hover over the stringers, showing no exposed screws. The stair is set against a wall clad in dramatic shou sugi ban, a Japanese charred cedar board. This impressive stair is also enclosed within glass panels up to twenty feet tall. They rise from the wine cellar, which serves as the extension of the entertainment area of the great room. Other custom features in this colossal space include built-in cabinets and custom light fixtures, designed by interior design firm Martine Paquin Design out of San Francisco.

One other part of the house that attracts considerable awe is the first-floor master bedroom within the angled double-height master suite wing. It is this private space that may be the most delightful room in the house. Every surface here is refined and beautifully put together. There is a white oak floor and a soaring 16-foot-tall ceiling clad in clear cedar. But what makes this space particularly impressive is its sculpturally attractive corner window that frames a stunning mountain view to the south. The two side walls that lead to the window are also quite special. The one on the bedside is all draped in textured gray fabric to provide the right acoustics, while the opposite wall features a full-height fireplace centered on the bed; it is finished in decorative concrete panels that both capture and reflect the natural light, intensifying spatial qualities of this generous and gorgeous space.

ANGLERS COURT

Steamboat Springs, Colorado, 2016 / 2019

Built in the company of large, generously spaced houses on either side of the namesake road in Steamboat Springs, Colorado, Anglers Court—a four-bedroom house—sits on the upper portion of a two-acre elongated lot that slopes down toward the south. This vacation house for a retired couple from Dallas—they spend about half of their time here—is a fusion of mountain contemporary and prairie styles, a disciplined version of some of the urban homes designed by Frank Lloyd Wright. Clad in clear cedar and stone veneer, it appears as a single-story residential compound from the front and turns into a two-story structure on the opposite downhill side where it offers uninterrupted 270-degree views of Mount Werner to the east, Steamboat Ski Resort to the south, and Emerald Mountain to the west.

The house, a timber structure, is composed of two main, roughly rectangular wings at the right angle to each other—double-story living quarters and a three-car garage with one space reserved for a large pickup truck. The two wings are linked by a mud/laundry room. The house is turned at a 45-degree angle to the street to maximize the aforementioned commanding views and to form a welcoming paved auto court framed by landscaped areas on both sides of a short curved driveway. The house is fragmented further into a cluster of interconnected orthogonal rooms topped by a system of low-pitched hipped roofs and canopies. Clad in dark-color metal shingles, the overlapped roofs are articulated with cedar soffits that match the façades' siding. A water feature cascades from the front of the property toward the back, filling several pools on its way down along the western part of the house, adding the presence of a serene sound. The south-facing façade is a handsome composition of stone elements interacting with wood posts and beams quite playfully.

The house is understated at the front to prepare visitors for expansive views through generous glazing in the back. It is centered on a great room, integrated into a large kitchen and dining area with the master bedroom and a guest bedroom on the main level. The central staircase sits under the tallest roof and connects to the recreation room and two single-bedroom suites downstairs. A wall of windows in the dining room blurs the distinction between indoor and outdoor living space, and radiant heat on the covered patio helps to extend the outdoor living season in the fleeting warmth of the mountain climate. The wood-paneled interior has a strong nod to some of the prairie-style houses by Wright and the detailing evokes the Arts and Crafts architecture by Greene and Greene. Among the most distinctive features of the interior is the prairie-style newel at the top of the stair with black oxide steel cable in the railing system. This house started a new design direction for Kelly|Stone Architects, exploring the prairie vernacular. It was the clients' love for the architects' hipped roof designs they explored in Hawaii that emboldened them to pursue this design direction here; the result is both distinctive and appropriate.

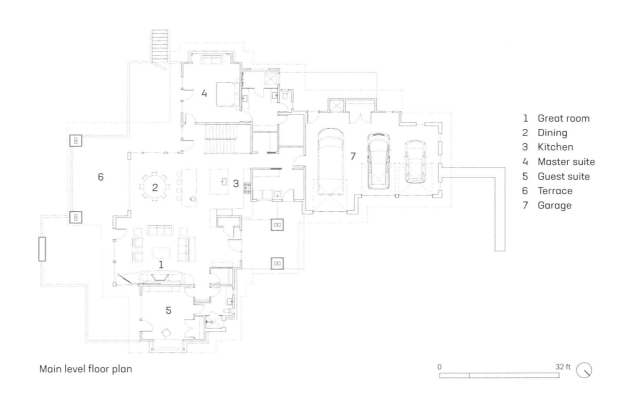

Main level floor plan

1 Great room
2 Dining
3 Kitchen
4 Master suite
5 Guest suite
6 Terrace
7 Garage

0   32 ft

HINMAN CREEK

Clark, Colorado, 2012

Located on a 70-acre wooded site at the foot of the Mount Zirkel Wilderness, about a forty-minute drive north of Steamboat Springs and near Hinman Park Campground, Hinman Creek is an extensive residential compound of several autonomous structures. The main house comprises a fan-shaped arrangement of four single-story and duplex orthogonal spaces, each topped by a gable roof and pivoting slightly from pointing to the northwest to the southeast. Rooms open toward forest views of Mount Zirkel Wilderness. Other parts of this property include a freestanding four-car garage with an exercise room above it, a subgrade wine cave on the cut side of the driveway with interior space of twenty feet by thirty feet under at least nine feet of earth, and additional structures a few hundred feet to the northeast—an eighty feet by 160 feet equestrian riding arena, an eight-stall barn, caretaker cabin, and repair shop. In addition to the detached garage, the main house, a four-bedroom home, incorporates another two-car garage with a state-of-the-art home theater above it.

The core of the house comprises a great room with a soaring twenty-five-foot-tall cathedral ceiling; it takes over its own volume with an extensive roof overhang and sculpturally expressed massive timber rafters and purlin extensions. A large kitchen and dining area are directly adjacent here and are covered by their own lower sloped ceiling that extends into a vast overhang above a sweeping outdoor terrace. Other common and private rooms and patios fit into and in between the other three volumes under a hierarchy of hefty gable roofs, sheds, and canopies held in place by a variety of trusses and supports.

Finished in 2012, Hinman Creek is the earliest project entirely designed by Kelly|Stone Architects—from exterior and interior to specifying all materials and developing every minute detail. The house is a unique ranch designed in mountain contemporary style and particularly distinguished for its expressive structural trusses both on the outside and within, dynamically assembled out of heavy timber chords and steel webs—square bars and tie rods. The house is clad in Montana limestone and sandstone from nearby Denver, reclaimed wood corral fence siding, and gable roofs are all covered in bonderized steel with matte zinc sulfate patina. The exuberant roofscape dynamically floats over extensive glazing, which is enabled by reinforced steel members. All first-floor rooms are accessible at grade level, effectively blurring the line between exterior and interior, particularly intensified by a babbling brook water feature, both seen and heard from within the master bedroom suite and common areas of the house.

Most interiors are characterized by the penetrating views of Big Agnes and Mount Farwell, an abundance of natural light, stone walls with traditional masonry fireplaces, and expansive woodwork overhead. The wood-and-steel trusses—a collaboration with Spearhead, a celebrated timber and steel fabricator out of Canada—make up a proud display of elements that evoke kinetic sculptures accented by dramatic lighting. The subgrade wine cave and a wine cellar, which are accessible from the great room foyer, attest to the owners'—an executive couple at a prominent microelectronics company in San Diego—great passion for collecting rare wines. Additionally, the architects oversaw the making of several intricate artworks—a multilayer glass panel over the main fireplace in the great room and a large stone panel mounted on a foyer wall like an abstract painting.

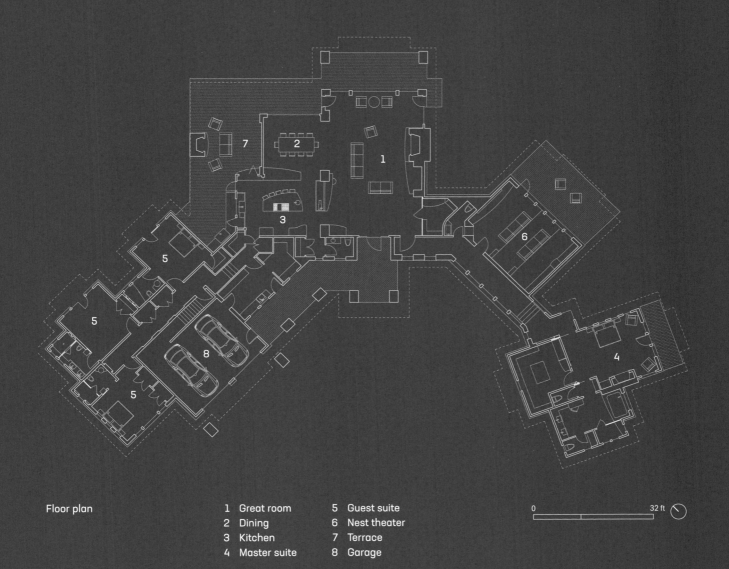

Floor plan

1 Great room
2 Dining
3 Kitchen
4 Master suite
5 Guest suite
6 Nest theater
7 Terrace
8 Garage

0   32 ft

PEARL STREET

Steamboat Springs, Colorado, 2014 (stage 1) / 2016 (stage 2)

The Pearl Street house, located in the historical Brooklyn neighborhood on the west side of Yampa River near the Old Town district in Steamboat Springs, is unusual in several ways. For one, this eclectic house was built in two stages—a two-car garage with a two-bedroom accessory dwelling unit above was finished first. It served as a temporary home for a young couple. Once their twin boys were born, they expanded by building the main house on the opposite, western end, of a rectangular 7,000-square-foot urban lot that runs in the east-west direction. Secondly, the house was both designed and built by Tim Stone for his own family. In fact, the architect was personally involved in excavation, concrete work, framing, roofing, trim carpentry, door installation, laying out tiles, and electrical wiring. Finally, what eventually became the main family home followed an uncommon upside-down plan: three bedrooms on the ground floor, while the family space—a single large room with an eighteen-foot-high ceiling to the ridge—is pushed upstairs to take advantage of expansive views of Emerald Mountain and Mount Werner to the west. This compelling space is complemented by two large decks on the west and east ends to maximize outdoor living.

The exterior facing Pearl Street, which features symmetrical steep gable forms reflects the old town mountain vernacular. Both structures are assembled and clad in a variety of materials—a patchwork of reclaimed wood corral fence siding, bonderized steel, and cold-rolled steel left to rust—all inscribed into heavy timber framing and characteristic, exposed rafters under a hierarchy of roofs, terraces, and canopies. South roofs carry solar panels and essentially bring the electric bill to zero. Speaking of this home's energy performance, it would be apt to mention here its excellent thermal efficiency enabled by triple-glazed windows and continuous insulation; both dramatically reduce energy usage. The naturally ventilated home has a heat recovery ventilator that delivers fresh air to the interior spaces without the need to rely on air conditioning.

It is the house's interior—particularly its spatial generosity, attractive materials, and neat details—that make this place among the nicest homes in its neighborhood. The interior design is driven by the exposed timber roof structure. A long ridge beam sits on two structural members oriented in the other direction and further rests on two parallel chord trusses that run the entire forty-five-foot length of the house. They are held by a system of interior columns that branch out with pairs of brackets that evoke raised arms. The chords are assembled out of upright timber supports and diagonal steel ties; they are outfitted with track lighting on the bottom, interrupted only by columns.

There is nothing decorative about this house's interior; all elements fulfill structural requirements. Nothing is covered up or glued to the structure to make it pretty. It is what it is, and the result is quite genuine. On the other hand, the space is used to display the architect's extensive collection of objects such as masks and pottery, which he and his wife brought from countless trips around the world. The display is peppered with some old family artifacts, ranging from propeller blades, snowshoes, tapestries, and a giant clam (*Tridacna gigas*) shell to a big whale vertebra. The interior was designed with these rare artifacts in mind from the start; they are carefully arranged in specially designed display cases and each object has its own spot to celebrate its oddity and beauty. Tim's photographs—a hobby he is devoted to since college—are a prominent part of the collection. At the time of writing, the architect is building a larger home for his family in Strawberry Park Hot Springs, situated north of Steamboat Springs.

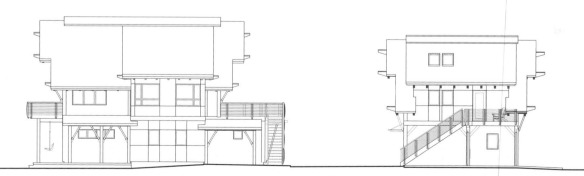

Upper level floor plan

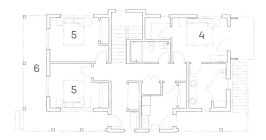

Main level floor plan

1   Living room
2   Dining
3   Kitchen
4   Master suite
5   Guest suite
6   Terrace
7   Garage

0   32 ft

NORTH ROUTT RETREAT

Clark, Colorado, 2012

Built for a Dutch couple who shares their time between New Haven, Connecticut, and the Steamboat Springs area, North Routt Retreat is a 3,500-square-foot sprawling compound made up of two detached structures—the main house and a three-car garage with an exercise room above. This ranch-style vacation home sits on a gently sloped, park-like 50-acre site in the Murphy-Larsen Ranch, just north of Clark, Colorado, and to the west of the majestic Mount Zirkel Wilderness area and Elk River. The area features aspen trees and Gambel oak and is surrounded by cattle ranches and thousands of acres of National Forest with an extensive network of picturesque nature trails. The main house, oriented in a southwest-northeast direction, comprises three wings, connected by neck-like narrow enclosed hallways. In profile, the asymmetrical composition mimics the mountain range around it and blends in quite naturally. The larger central wing is made up of a living room with an open stair to a single bedroom above, a kitchen, dining area, foyer, mud/laundry room, and pantry. The two other wings are single-story; one is a master suite, while the other is a guest suite. The entire house is built over a crawlspace and mechanical equipment spaces.

The house is a rambling Douglas fir timber-frame structure. It is reminiscent of American agricultural barns, but with overexaggerated profiles and overtly expressed structural members—extended, elongated, leaned, crisscrossed, and overlapped, resulting in unusually dynamic, even sculptural profiles and somewhat heroic forms. Yet, the relaxed, spread-out winged plan affords southeast views toward Mount Zirkel Wilderness from every bedroom, while multiple adjacent terraces create a variety of outdoor living opportunities.

recycled Wyoming snow fence, and weathered steel panel siding, while the roofs are all oxidized metal with a rust patina. All exterior soffits and decking are of local lodgepole pine. Among the most memorable design features are the front split columns, each turning into a double sculptural expression, precariously supporting beams directly above, and outriggers either deeply projecting forward or to the sides; each is slightly different from its neighbors. These sculptural elements express the house's artistic identity, which reflects the architect's engagement with the material itself rather than imitating any design precedents.

Expectedly, the house's interior is primarily made of wood with inserted structural steel elements such as stair stringers and dynamically expressed bottom chords and ties that are aligned into an impressive array of asymmetrical trusses. One central element that draws particular attention is a wood-burning stove. It sits like a treasured museum artifact on a very large and thick stone cap against a stone wall reinforced by a couple of steel beams. This conversation piece is paired with another outdoor fireplace directly behind it, on a welcoming porch under a shed roof.

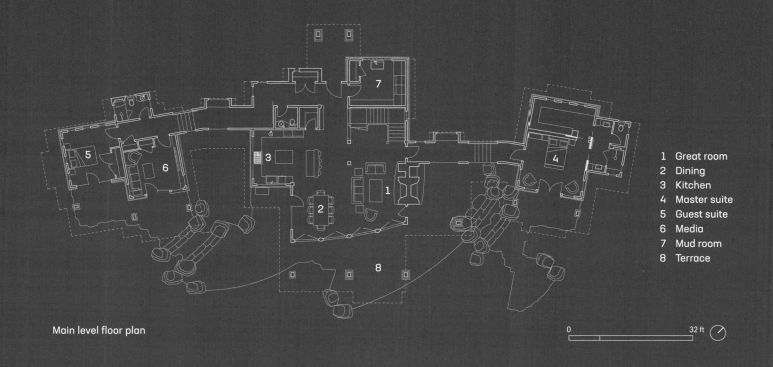

1   Great room
2   Dining
3   Kitchen
4   Master suite
5   Guest suite
6   Media
7   Mud room
8   Terrace

Main level floor plan

0   32 ft

SWIFTS STATION

Carson City, Nevada, 2019

Swifts Station sits on a steep two-acre site at the Clear Creek Tahoe development known for its all-encompassing gorgeous mountain views. The property is accessed from the high side with a curved driveway leading to a paved rectangular auto court in front of a large L-shaped house that hugs it on two sides. A three-car garage fits within the short bar of the L, while the main house forms its long bar. Oriented in a southwest-northeast direction, the main house is a single-story structure at the front; it doubles with an additional lower floor on the opposite view side. Volumetrically, this five-bedroom home is defined by four soaring curves—three over the dwelling's top floor and one over the garage; these roofs are curved in the direction of each of the two bars. Thin and well-proportioned, these airy elements form curved ceilings that are meant to bring the outdoors in and capture the beauty of the surrounding treetops and mountain peaks. All graciously raised on clerestories, they are connected by a series of flat roof segments topped by pebbles.

The main floor comprises a central great room, kitchen, and dining area with one bedroom suite on the garage side and a master bedroom suite with an office at the opposite end. The auto court and the living quarters are separated by a linear water and landscape feature. This means that to gain access to the house, guests need to cross a specially designed bridge that connects to a formal entry to the great room, a broad space under an eighteen-foot-high curved ceiling embracing uninterrupted scenic views of the Carson Range directly ahead.

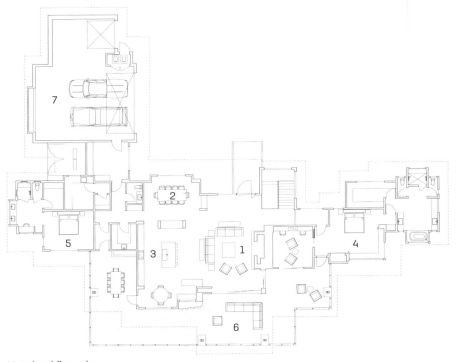

Main level floor plan

1 Great room
2 Dining
3 Kitchen
4 Master suite
5 Guest suite
6 Terrace
7 Garage
8 Golf simulator

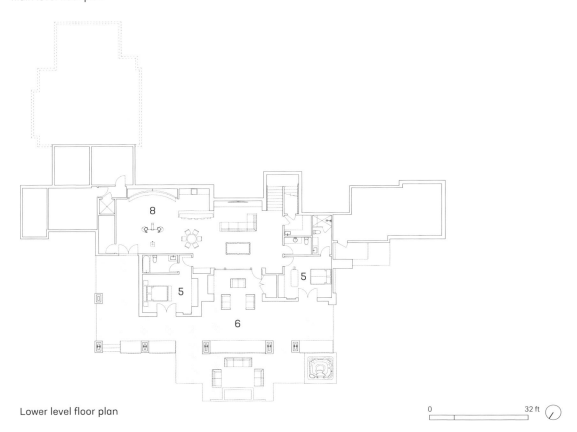

Lower level floor plan

0 _____ 32 ft

The decision to employ curved roofs in this project—a rare alternative to Kelly|Stone Architects' typical use of gable and shed designs—was specifically requested by the clients who fell in love with a curved roof house they came across. Seemingly floating above clerestories, the resultant softly curved airy forms work well with extensive clear glazing and skillfully selected exterior building materials such as exposed poured-in-place concrete walls, stone-clad piers, aluminum composite panel siding system with concealed fasteners, areas of clear cedar and mahogany, as well as bonderized steel with a natural zinc patina finish. To take advantage of the mild climate, the dwelling incorporates spacious outdoor elevated decks and such design features as a pass-through bar into the kitchen and a multipanel lift-slide door in the great room. The interiors are consistent with the exteriors, which are characterized by the abundance of cedar and other wood surfaces, mainly ceilings, and highlighted by stone-clad piers.

The great room is particularly memorable for its single, large truss—a dynamic array of steel web plates and ties that connect the massive top and bottom wood chords. Not only does this truss support the roof, but it also serves as an artistic artifact proudly put on a prominent display for everyone to admire. A stair volume, positioned between the great room and master bedroom suite and two adjacent curved roofs leads down to the lower floor with a recreation area that includes a bar, media space, billiards, and additional bedroom suites for guests, fronted with extensive terraces with planters and surrounded by lawns and landscaped areas, all presiding over magnificent views that stretch from the southeast to the southwest.

Swifts Station is one of the first vacation homes built at the Clear Creek Tahoe development where owners share such amenities as golf and a swimming pool at a multifunctional amenities center. This fact enabled the clients, a couple from Texas, to scrap the original plan of building their own infinity-edge pool. Several other special features that are worth mentioning here include a specially designed shading screen on the façade in front of the dining area and onyx light cylinders over the dining table, both designed by the architect. Recently, following the couple's divorce, the house was placed on the market. At the time of writing, four other Kelly|Stone Architects-designed houses—all within a stone's throw of this exemplary structure—are under construction.

BARN VILLAGE

Steamboat Springs, Colorado, 2020

Located within just a few minutes' driving distance from Kelly|Stone Architects' office, Barn Village is a vacation home that sits on a compact beautiful site in the heart of a popular Fish Creek home development in Steamboat Springs. This densely built residential area has grown along and around Fish Creek, a scenic stream that comes down nimbly from Fish Creek Falls about five miles to the east in Routt National Forest. The three-level house faces a T-intersection to the south and directly overlooks Fish Creek to the north. From upstairs there are also views of Steamboat Ski Resort and Mountain Werner to the east. Tim Stone designed several other homes for this development and, according to the architect, Barn Village is the most remarkable house here, as far as its special attention to detail and high-quality workmanship. Exterior materials are dominated by wood and mixed blocky limestone blend, as well as emblematic of Kelly|Stone Architects' extensive glazing, all topped by a pair of steep gable forms interconnected by a system of gently sloped roofs. Two chimneys at the east and west ends of the house are clad in fiber cement panels; they appear like matte metal in their attempt to match the dark metal finish of the interior fireplaces.

Fairly reserved at the front and partially obstructed by a semidetached two-car garage, the house presents itself quite theatrically on its private north-facing side where a curved stone stair that spectacularly descends from the main-level master bedroom to the grade, at the lower floor-level, is accompanied by a rich arrangement of boulders and linked stone-paved patios. Other highlights here include a heated Jacuzzi and a couple of multitone boulders that complement well the naturally scattered boulders in Fish Creek, virtually in this home's backyard.

The house is accessed either from the two-car garage via the mudroom or through a formal foyer in the west wing, which comprises a great room with a bar and fireplace under a 14-foot cathedral wood ceiling with massive triangular trusses, kitchen and dining area under a sloped wooden ceiling, pantry room, and an open stair volume connecting to two additional floors—the lower level with two guest bedroom suites and a lounge and the upper level with office/bedroom suite with a terrace on the garage side. The west wing living-dining area leads to the north-facing elevated deck with a barbecue grill and gas fireplace overlooking Fish Creek. The interiors are largely finished in a mixed blocky limestone blend, hardwood floors, cedar ceilings, and blackened steel highlight elements such as the entire stair structure and railings, as well as waxed hot-rolled steel on a curved vent hood over the kitchen stove.

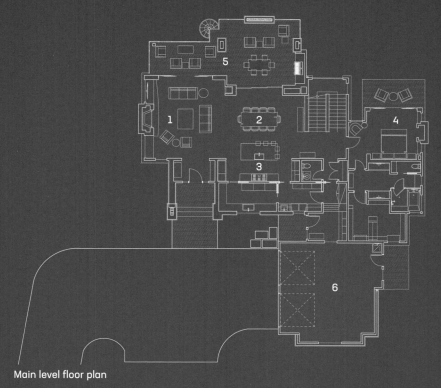

Main level floor plan

1 Great room
2 Kitchen
3 Dining
4 Master suite
5 Terrace
6 Garage
7 Guest suite
8 Bunk room
9 Media room

Lower level floor plan

0   32 ft

One of the most curious elements in the house is a massive double beam, the support for the west gable situated between the living room and the kitchen-dining area. With a special connection between the two stacked beams that work like one—a series of hardwood keys keep them from sliding. Such heavy, old English, timber detail with as many as four stacked beams sometimes is used in buildings but it is quite uncommon to encounter it in residential construction. All interiors were designed by the architect, while the owners, a couple from Pennsylvania, involved an Amish cabinet fabricator to produce all the furniture here, all coordinated by the architect.

RADIUM HOT SPRINGS

Radium Hot Springs, British Columbia, 2014

Radium Hot Springs is a six-bedroom family cabin that sits solemnly on a nearly flat wooded lot of a 50-acre range on the margin of aspen and spruce-fir forest in the Purcell Mountains of eastern British Columbia. The mountain getaway, built for a Calgary-based client, a large excavation company owner, is the second house that Tim Stone designed for this businessman. The first one was the primary residence in Calgary. Although that house followed a more-traditional design approach, it was the client's intention, here in the mountains, to pursue a much more open-ended and unmistakably contemporary architecture with a strong focus on expressing timber and steel structural components. The house is a relaxed, unfolding composition of scattered pavilions assembled into a family of interconnected forms under low-slung, deeply projected, shed roofs. Presiding over a lush meadow, each volume that at first may seem to be randomly placed, in fact, negotiates quite precisely the best possible relationship to predominantly southern views toward the Bugaboos, the mountains known for their distinctive granite spires.

Characterized by extensive glazing, framed by cedar shiplap with gray metal panels, the house's mainly single-story volumes are neatly gathered around a large, two-story, central structure with a great room under a soaring eighteen-foot ceiling. These volumes of the somewhat restricted palette of materials and colors are particularly distinctive for their sculpturally expressed pairs of unequal exterior columns that hold greatly extended inclined roof overhangs, thrusting forward and upward to capture maximum light and views. These uncommon extensions put on display their exposed framework of girders, rafters, beams, and occasional bowstring trusses to achieve extra strength and project a strong character. At night this tree-crown-like filigree is intricately lit.

A couple of tapered and limestone-clad chimneys gracefully tower over this house's rhythmic roofscape. The tree-like frontal columns stand out for their complex assemblies; each is put together out of load-bearing back-to-back steel channels with a sandwiched timber member and a knee brace to support deeply extended roof overhangs. These sturdy columns, none exactly the same, make the entire structure quite airy, even organic looking and creature-like.

The "three-headed" house comprises a casual central vestibule that leads to the central great room, branching out into a master bedroom suite on one side and a cluster of four other bedrooms—three small ones with a shared bathroom, and a junior master bedroom suite on the other. An open stair next to the great room leads upstairs to an additional bedroom with bunk beds for kids. All interiors feature reclaimed Douglas fir flooring and cedar ceilings with exposed timber framing and arrays of sculpturally expressed bowstring trusses. A large, muscular, composite wood-and-steel truss positioned right on the border between the great room and dining area is responsible for providing a column-free space that fortifies the structure to combat huge snow accumulation on the roof.

Floor plan

1 Great room
2 Dining
3 Kitchen
4 Master suite
5 Jr master suite
6 Bedroom
7 Bathroom
8 Mudroom
9 Patio

0   32 ft

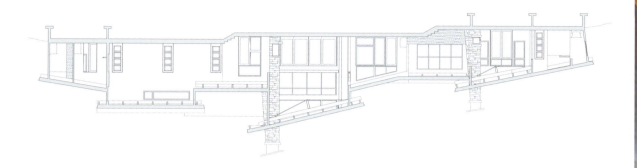

One of the most characteristic design features in this house is the presence of several rammed earth walls. This ancient building technique, revived and mastered by experimental home builders in recent years, was employed here to bring the artistic touch and highly skilled craftsmanship to the domestic environment. It also underlines the strong link to nature all around. These remarkable walls serve as special highlights in the great room, foyer, and most prominently, the master bedroom. Constructed with local soil, lime, gravel, and other natural raw materials, the achieved subtle color variations evoke the likeliness of abstract paintings. They add rich texture and enhance soundproofing.

Although some remote influences on this house's design may be attributed to such great American architects as Frank Lloyd Wright or E. Fay Jones, it is clear that the key governing ideas and forms come straight from the site itself and the nature that surrounds it. While the asymmetrical fractured rooftine profile mimics the mountain range to the north, the aspen-tree forest in front of it and all around inspired the architect to bring individual characters to such elements as trusses, columns, accent walls, ledges, and overhangs throughout this striking dwelling.

Walls around fireplaces in the great room and master bedroom are clad from floor to ceiling in ledge limestone sourced from a local quarry. Kitchen cabinets are made of hard and durable rift-cut white oak. This is an abundance of wood, stone, and steel structural elements—all convey warmth and coziness throughout the house, while extensive glazing succeeds in blurring clear distinctions between interior and exterior spaces.

KAHALAWAI

Koloa, Hawaii, 2017

Kahalawai, a contemporary tropical-style house, is one of the earliest homes built in Kukui'ula, a resort community on the sunny and dry South Shore of the fourth largest island in Hawaii, Kauai. A former sugar plantation, this exclusive development is not only known for its beautiful setting—over 300 days of sunshine—and a wide range of amenities but also for its superb architecture, particularly stunning cottages and villas along hillside slopes and ocean overlooks. These noble Pacific Tropical-style houses are designed as a direct response to the local climate and take advantage of available materials and building technology. Inspired by some of the most celebrated examples of the Hawaiian post-war modernist period, many of these houses are designed by such internationally renowned architects as Shay Zak, Olson Kundig, and Bing Hu.

Kelly|Stone Architects had a very strong presence starting from the early days of this development and Keith Kelly has been serving as a consultant for creating local guidelines that refer to traditional plantation-style houses but also encourage homeowners to be more contemporary and experimental architecturally. Kelly also sits on the development's reviews board. Over the years, he designed and built at least a dozen homes in different parts of Kukui'ula, and he is involved in the design of some of the public amenities here. Kahalawai has served well as a model for many subsequent homes in the resort, as it comprises all the most desirable features of an exemplary local home: a compact cluster of hipped-roof symmetrical pavilions, airy interiors, an abundance of natural materials, and permeability between interiors and exteriors to celebrate a well-balanced indoor-outdoor lifestyle.

The Kelly-designed home sits on one of the most advantageous sites in Kukui'ula, about half a mile away from the shore. It is situated close to the highest elevation point of the community and takes advantage of its breathtaking hillside setting with unobstructed wide panoramic views of the deep-blue ocean to the southwest and of lush mountains to the northeast. The house tops the upper portion of a steep site formed into a cascade of flat landscaped linear terraces interconnected by stairs. The simple hipped-roof single- and double-story pavilion forms are gathered around the great room that comprises the kitchen, living, and dining areas. Two master suites—one with the ocean view and the other with the mountain view, both connected with the lounge—are directly attached to it forming their own wing. Four additional guest bedrooms are situated upstairs above the two master suites and on the opposite end of the house.

The hipped-roof pavilions are connected with flat-roofed circulation spaces enclosed by large expanses of glass. On the mountainside with the main entry and driveway, the house seems to grow right out of the basalt stone plaza and walkways defined by lush landscaping and low walls made of volcanic stone. These stones are imported from Asia, but they are indicative of what would be used here traditionally. The transparent nature of the house allows visitors to see the ocean on the opposite side right away, as the airy interiors interact with reliably blue water and sky. Throughout the house, interiors constantly intermingle with the outdoor spaces. Both are clad in clear cedar and locally sourced volcanic stone and cut puka lava. These tropical materials were selected for their ability to withstand harsh environmental conditions and blend with the surrounding landscape. Windows, ceilings, light coves, and cabinets are all made of Afromosia, a type of Indonesian tropical wood. The soaring great room features sliding doors that reach a height of eleven feet and ceiling heights range from fourteen to eighteen feet at the ridge.

On the private ocean-view side of the house, the key central feature is a large, rectangular, infinity-edge pool on all four sides. Elevated above the top terrace with its water surface hovering about a foot over the floor level of the house, it blends with the ocean in the distance and reflects the sky above. The pool's dominating physical presence also brings a constant sound of trickling water to the great room and adjacent spaces. The piece serves as a culmination of a series of cascading waterfalls and interconnected channels floating under the entryway designed like a bridge, bringing visitors in gently, between rooms and gardens. All interiors are entirely custom with such exquisitely crafted accent pieces as cabinets and the wine bar. Expressive furniture pieces hold the center stage here in their own right. Curved sofas, eye-catching chairs, and strikingly dynamic tables are all inspired by mid-twentieth century Hawaiian modern design, while decorative wall coverings add a touch of palm desert aesthetics.

The client for this delightful house, a Palm Springs resident, was the founder of a successful company called International Game Technology, which is responsible for the crucial technology behind making all slot machines turn. Following his recent passing, the house was sold to new owners who are fond of its compelling design and are committed to maintaining it.

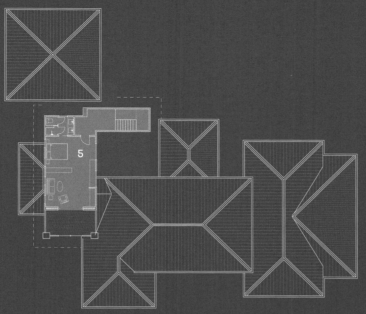

Upper level floor plan

1   Great room
2   Dining
3   Kitchen
4   Master suite
5   Guest suite
6   Bunk room
7   Media room
8   Terrace
9   Garage
10 Pool

Main level floor plan

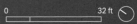

0   32 ft

COPELAND LANE

Truckee, California, 2012

Truckee, California has been home to Kelly|Stone Architects since 2012, when Keith Kelly relocated here to open the firm's second office. And it is not surprising that several houses in this book are located in the Lake Tahoe region. Copeland Lane was the first house the architects designed and built in California; it became the reason for opening their second office here. The house is among the architects' earliest and largest projects and it couldn't come at a better time—during the recession of 2007-8 when most of its design work was carried out. The house was commissioned by a divorced businesswoman with three grown children; together they manage a multibillion real estate empire in San Francisco. The entire family, which includes many grandchildren, spends vacations in this house— often all at once. Curiously, the transitional styling of this sumptuous home reflects the individual preferences of the four family members, who were all actively involved in the design process.

Copeland Lane is situated in the Martis Camp, a private community of luxury mountain homes; it encompasses over 2,000 acres of a densely wooded area in Placer County, California with generously spaced cabin and estate sites that range from one-third to two acres. The house sits near the golf course and the community lodge with such amenities as a bowling alley, swimming pool, tennis courts, and movie theaters. It commands a direct view of the primary peak of the Northstar California Resort, which is visible through gorgeous white pines and Jeffrey pines, as well as some sugar pines; these native trees are strenuously protected.

The three-story house is a six-bedroom compound, which includes a large bunk bedroom, of two semidetached wings—one with the formal entry, a great room, and most bedrooms, while the other one comprises a three-car garage and additional bedrooms upstairs. The front entry, right off a squarish paved auto court, is marked by an expressly curved timber canopy, a welcoming gesture coming out of stone walls and piers, and accented with steel plates, connections, and bolts. But it is the other side, overlooking the mountains, that's designed truly generously, even lavishly, both in terms of space and materials employed.

This characteristic façade is largely defined by the building's two intersecting roof features—a sweeping, concave-curved roof over the great room with a soaring, twenty-one-foot ceiling and the gable roof portico directly in front of it. These bold forms blend both modern sensibilities and rustic traditional mountain styles.

The main roof is complemented by a curved deck, adding a sense of lifting off toward fairytale-like mountain views. The portico's primary window measures eight feet by fourteen feet, which is the biggest piece of glass that could fit into a shipping container; all windows were brought in from Germany and are designed to withstand severe earthquakes and hurricanes. The home's outdoor spaces include a custom spa built into a specially designed stone landscape feature, a stone firepit, and a built-in bench on a heated raised deck.

The home's exterior is predominantly clad in stone and wood. Landscaped areas, the ground floor all around, many walls extending all the way to the roof, and chimneys are clad in ledge stone from Montana. It is selected for its rust color, which is composed of a mixture of a couple of different blends. Wood siding—reclaimed barn wood with gray tin—is used on the upper floor areas blending with extensive roof soffits. Rusted steel panels are laid horizontally to emulate wood and to better fit metal railings along terraces on the main floor. All these materials require no maintenance; they were selected to last for generations. The roofs' deeply projected overhangs are supported by expressive timber elements. All made of Douglas fir, they complement beautifully detailed trusses that are proudly put on display both from inside and outside through extensive glazing. The roofs are clad in zinc with a natural patina.

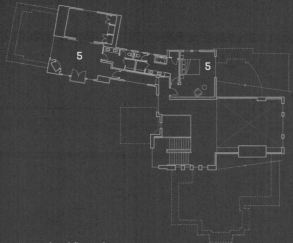

Upper level floor plan

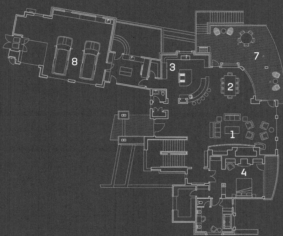

1 Great room
2 Dining
3 Kitchen
4 Master suite
5 Guest suite
6 Game room
7 Terrace
8 Garage

Main level floor plan

Lower level floor plan

0 ⊏⊐⊏⊐ 32 ft

Many of the exterior materials were brought inside, especially stone, which makes up many of the walls on the main level, particularly in the kitchen area. Wood is the other dominating material here—wall panels, doors, walnut floors, stairs, handrails, and virtually everything overhead: exposed beams, trusses, soffits, and vaulted ceilings. All cabinets are also walnut with accent pieces in different materials. Cabinetry and concealed storage areas are thoughtfully integrated into bedrooms and other living spaces to accommodate the needs of this growing multigenerational family. Handcrafted mahogany and glass windows deliver panoramic mountain and forest views from all rooms. Interiors were planned around many of the art pieces and artifacts that the family acquired specifically for this house in their extensive travels with custom-designed lighting to highlight these treasures.

CARSON VISTA

Truckee, California, 2017

Located along the wooded slopes of Martis Camp, a private community of luxury mountain homes just south of Truckee, California, Carson Vista stands out for its rigorous geometry and material palette, and the way it is integrated into its steep site. It is Tim Stone's favorite work designed by Keith Kelly who did quite a few houses in this development; some are included in this book. It is the site itself—its challenging topography alone would easily scare most homeowners and builders—that provoked the architect to undertake such a unique and, above all, disciplined response. The house, which is neatly organized along a series of ledges between the retaining walls at the bottom and at the top, is deeply cut into the hillside. There is something resolutely abstract about this project—a pattern of perfectly horizontal and vertical lines and planes intersecting each other in midair, evoking an intriguing De Stijl painting. Projecting out in all directions, consistently at the right angle, these hefty orthogonal forms are clad predominantly in four contrasting materials: light-color Quartzite ledge stone, all-natural redwood cedar, prefinished blackened steel panels, and large expanses of clear glass. They appear to be pure volumes and planes rather than façades, roofs, windows, chimneys, and other familiar features of domestic architecture. Nevertheless, the result is a well-balanced contemporary dwelling characterized by warm materiality and sleek geometry. This compelling combination makes the house appear simultaneously traditional and modern.

Carson Vista is owned by a repeat client who is open to innovative solutions and it was the architect who helped to find him this site. Curiously, the client owns a construction company that was responsible for building this and several other houses, also designed by Kelly, all in this part of the country. Architecturally, this project is inspired by Frank Lloyd Wright's prairie-style houses that proudly thrust forward their seemingly perfectly flat and lengthy cantilevers over extensive glazing; here cantilevers extend up to eighteen feet. It should be noted that these dramatic overhangs are further exacerbated by the fact that snow in this area stays for at least six months every year, accumulating up to six to eight feet, and staying for months before melting. Yet the real feat of engineering here is accomplished by concealing all structural elements into the walls. This means that the primary double roof structure is entirely supported by the central stone fireplace and cantilevered roofs are held in place by a system of stone walls. In fact, there are no freestanding columns or braces—not outside, nor inside.

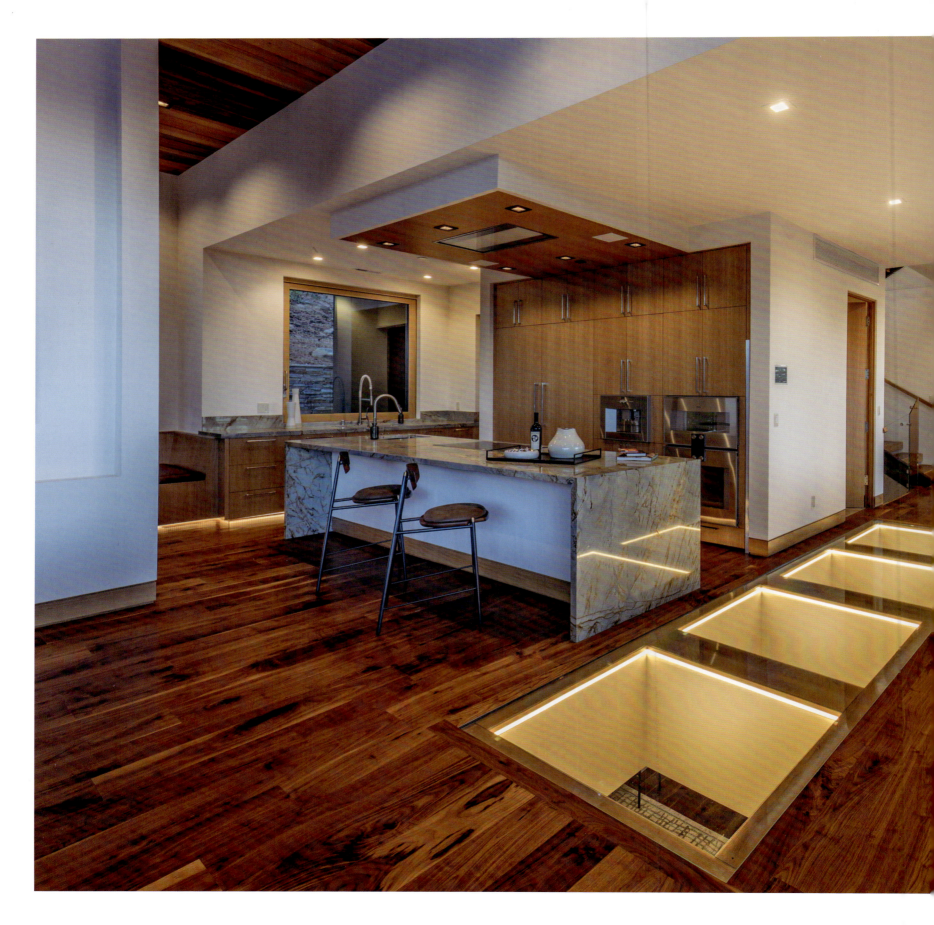

The house rises over four levels of rectangular rooms and spaces—all staggered and shifted—to take maximum advantage of the expansive mountain views in front of it. The six-bedroom house includes a low-level three-car garage, media room, a gym, a home theater, an office, a great room with fourteen-foot-high flat ceiling, and lots of terraces. But what makes this house even more unique spatially and experientially is its magical ability to open its many corners. This trick is achieved through the use of six sliding pocket corner door systems—three of them are employed in the grate room alone—to bring unobstructed mountain and forest views right in and blend indoors and outdoors on every level. The effect makes the house appear boundless and weightless.

The same materials that distinguish this house from the outside are brought inside—Quartzite ledge stone wall accents, walnut floors, built-in custom cabinets, and cedar soffits that connect seemingly seamlessly with the cedar-clad roof overhangs to further fuse the indoor-outdoor spaces. Among the spaces and features of note, we need to mention the two-story entryway that helps to connect the lower and main levels. It conveys a sense of arrival and connection to the main level. All levels are linked by a floating steel staircase, a sculptural element that entices visitors upstairs. An elevator with windows and doors that open on different sides, provides an alternative means of vertical navigation. Finally, four structural-glass skylights built into the main floor open the lower level, a striking feature, and a hint for those who just arrived that this house is more than a fancy dwelling; rather, it is an inhabited sculpture.

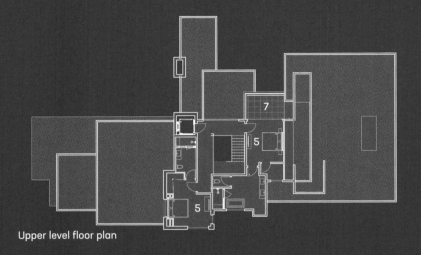

Upper level floor plan

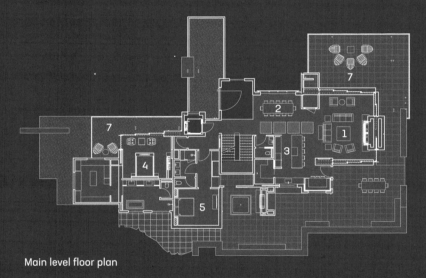

Main level floor plan

Lower level floor plan

1   Great room
2   Dining
3   Kitchen
4   Master suite
5   Guest suite
6   Media room
7   Terrace
8   Garage

HALE 'O LUNA O KA LĀLA

Kauai, Hawaii, 2018

While many Kelly|Stone-designed houses are tied directly to the local context such as topography, preferred views, the sun path, and prevailing winds, and conditioned by climate and clients' living standards and preferences, occasionally, they are inspired by architectural precedents. In this case, the point of departure came from the client's inquiry into the work of Russian-born American architect Vladimir Ossipoff (1907–98), the master of Hawaiian modern architecture who is referred to as the dean of residential architects in Hawaii. The extensive research included a visit to one of Ossipoff's masterpieces, the Liljestrand House (1952) in Honolulu; meeting with the original owner's son; and exchanging ideas with Dean Sakamoto, an architect, professor at the University of Hawaii, and an expert on Ossipoff's architecture. This immersion in the meaning, history, and design of the Classic mid-century modern Hawaiian home is reflected strongly in this house by Keith Kelly, which became an important transition in the architect's own aesthetics, previously dominated by his experience of building in the mountainous areas of California and Colorado. Working on this project diversified the firm's prevalent vernacular and brought new sensibilities to their work both in Hawaii and elsewhere.

Hale 'o Luna O Ka Lāla is a vacation home for a multigenerational family. It occupies a unique elevated lot on a steep slope going down toward the ocean to the south. Naturally accessed from the top on the single-story north side, the house's double-height façade opens due south where it borders and overlooks the community orchard with a variety of fruit trees and a vegetable garden down below.

The setting allows 180-degree uninterrupted panoramic ocean views. It was one of the earliest houses built in Kukui'Ula, a former sugar plantation that closed in the early 1990s and sold for development. This large community on the south shore of Kauai island now numbers close to one thousand luxury houses. The house was designed for the family of the community's original developer who also wanted it to serve as a demonstration model to showcase Hawaiian architecture—modern, yet with a traditional feeling to it. It was meant to be tailored toward younger demographics with families, a change in the area, which used to be popular with older retirees with more conservative tastes. In the past, only traditional plantation homes were allowed to be built in this area.

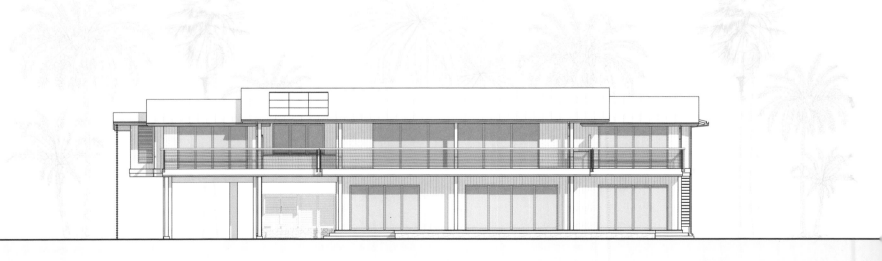

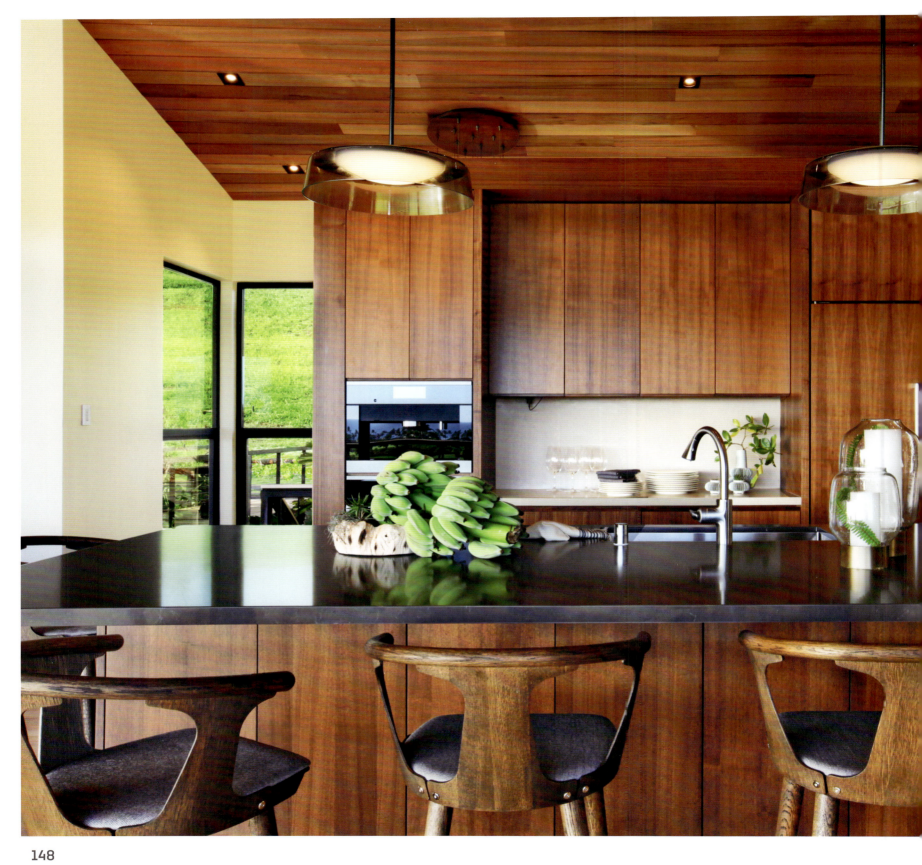

What makes this house unusual among other projects designed by Kelly|Stone Architects is its overall compactness and straightforwardness—a double-height orthogonal domestic volume stretches along the east-west axis, perpendicular to the direction of the slope, and has an attached double-deep garage at the front side of the west end; it provides generous space for storing bikes, and other recreational gear. The house's vertical configuration is somewhat uncommon for this area, as most neighboring homes are designed as single-story residences. A straight driveway runs along the east-west direction along the upper border of the site and parallels the house directly below it. The driveway is made of special stained concrete with inserted rocks and grass strips in a geometric pattern—tying into lava formations used in the design of the house. The main upper floor is accessed by a covered bridge that brings visitors to a large gabled living room/dining area; it is flanked by identical guest suites. All rooms directly spill out onto a deep continuous terrace on the south side. This floor sits on an array of wooden stilts while its eastern end looms over a much shorter lower floor with two guest bedroom suites on either side of a secondary living room used as an entertainment area; all rooms on this level open to an expansive outdoor seating area framing a rectangular pool.

The ceiling heights here are relatively low—ten feet in most spaces on the main floor and nine feet downstairs to maintain the local tradition of providing comfortable human scale and shade. In the great room the cathedral ceiling peaks at fourteen feet. This open living area with heavy timber trusses is defined by a rustic fireplace at one end and a custom kitchen range unit at the other. Both are crafted of locally sourced granite. The architects worked on cabinet design throughout the house while a local designer selected most materials and finishes.

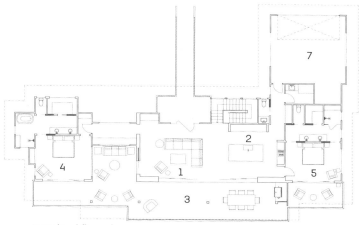

Main level floor plan

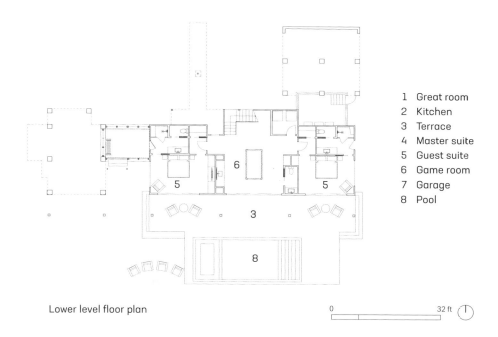

1   Great room
2   Kitchen
3   Terrace
4   Master suite
5   Guest suite
6   Game room
7   Garage
8   Pool

Lower level floor plan

0 _____ 32 ft

The house touches the land quite gently. From some vantage points, it appears almost floating by exposing its underbelly and allowing lush greenery to poke through all around it. The standing seam metal roof is traditionally pitched but the way skylights with inserted semitransparent solar panels are incorporated makes it quite sleek and contemporary. Passive ventilation and cooling principles are pushed to the maximum here and operable windows, some of which are frosted or composed of glass blades for privacy, create an effective and pleasant airflow throughout the house. Materials are mainly clear cedar, which is decay and insect-resistant. It is treated to make it match redwood, which was the preferred material by Ossipoff but is no longer an option. Lava stone, a locally sourced native stone, is used in various places in the house. The entry bridge, interior flooring, outdoor decks, and walkways are paved in clear teak wood slabs and there are accent areas on walls and floors made of imported Turkish limestone. The house showcases both traditional and contemporary techniques that are masterfully woven together.

Finally, the house's most exquisite and chic design feature is the open stair that connects two living rooms on the northern side between the entry and garage. It is set within an enclosure with a windowed northern wall with lush greenery outside. The sculptural stair is distinguished by massive floating treads and characteristic steel cables. It is inspired by Ossipoff's open riser stair at his aforementioned Liljestrand House. The architects worked with local craftsmen to achieve remarkable precision and refinement.

E KOMO MAI

Koloa, Hawaii, 2022

E Komo Mai presides quite nobly over an elevated field of lush greenery, looking down at a nearby landscaped garden area and extensive scenic southern views toward the Pacific Ocean. The house, largely symmetrical in plan and formed into a group of three interconnected pavilion-like structures with distinctive roofs, is situated between two fairways of the Kukui'ula Golf Course in the heart of Kukui'Ula development on the south shore of the island of Kauai. The imposing home sits just above another Kelly|Stone-designed house, Hale 'o Luna O Ka Lāla, included in this book. The one-acre property is accessed from a driveway tacked into the northeastern corner of the site. It cuts across and along the front of the house bringing visitors to a compact paved central auto court. A three-car garage with gear storage is attached to the house's northwestern corner.

The house is entered from the auto court via an off-centered bridge over an elongated planter; it leads directly to the great room-dining area and kitchen, cutting straight between a lanai—a regional porch—and a similarly sized planter with a central water feature. Both the frontal lanai and planter are surrounded by low stone walls to minimize the prevailing northeastern winds. These front-door outdoor spaces are provided in addition to much larger recreational areas in the back in response to the occasional wind coming from the southwest. On the south side in the back, the house is fortified by a series of long terraced walls clad in stacked lava stone veneer, and garden areas to better accommodate this steep property.

The centrally located great room features an uncommonly high twenty-foot vaulted ceiling and a wall of dark bronze metal pocket doors that fold away to the sides, leaving a broad south-facing wall entirely open. This central tall space is flanked by two visually well-balanced zones—a cluster of three adjacent bedroom suites comprising the west wing and a spacious master bedroom that constitutes its own wing at the east end. The west volume includes one additional top-floor bedroom/office with an outdoor terrace. The spacious great room flows out to an expansive rear terrace that includes an elevated infinity-edge pool and entertainment space with a built-in barbecue and serving area. All bedrooms on the ground floor have their own lanais paved in basalt tile. They are all connected with gardens and lawns with lava gravel and puka lava steppingstone accents. One special design element—a bridge-like breezeway with sculptural water features on both sides—connects the great room with the master bedroom, bringing a feeling of blurred indoor-outdoor connection deep inside the house. The master bedroom is distinguished by glass walls on three sides and a decorative ceiling fabric.

The structure of the house is made of cedar posts and beams and conventional wood framing. The exterior is dominated by clear/select vertical cedar siding with sikken's cetol "cedar" finish and all roofs are clad in cedar shake. Lots of refined timberwork with exposed timber rafters are designed in response to traditional Hawaiian houses and incorporate contemporary wood frame techniques and insulation. Many features throughout the house, such as an intricately carved entry door and coral stone veneer accent walls reflect the heritage of the client's wife who is originally from South America, manifesting in a unique fusion of Hawaiian architecture and South American influences. The client, an investment manager, spends time with his family evenly between living here on the island of Kauai and on Lake Tahoe, at another house, also designed by Kelly|Stone Architects.

KINGSCOTE COURT

Truckee, California, 2019

Kingscote Court is a large, three-story, sprawling vacation home that sits on a gently sloped 1.6-acre wooded site elongated along the north-south axis within Martis Camp, a private ski and golf community of custom-designed cabins and estates just south of Truckee, California. Forbes once called this luxury development, "Possibly the best four-season community in the U.S." The house is composed of orthogonal volumes propped up on timber posts and stone-clad walls; they carry a series of pitched metal roofs protruded by lofty chimney stacks. These volumes are interconnected and overlapped, making a coherent family of smaller forms further framed and outlined by multiple patios and low stone walls. Both inside and out, the building is a stylistic hybrid. It is characterized by traditional and contemporary features that coexist quite harmonically—rustic stone and wood surfaces under cathedral ceilings with small-sized windows on the one hand and refined wood and blackened steel areas, exposed structural elements, modern steel-clad light fixtures, appliances, and stylish furniture selection, and overall clean look—on the other.

These contrasting, yet well-matched choices reflect the tastes and sensibilities of the clients, a couple out of San Francisco. He is an American businessman who wanted to recreate a feeling of a sweet sheltering lodge on a lake that he remembers growing up in, and she is originally from Sweden with a strong fondness for Scandinavian sleek design and straight unadorned surfaces and lines. They own several other vacation houses in various parts of the world, but it is the Truckee property they are most attached to and consider home, and where the entire multigenerational family likes to gather frequently.

The house faces the practice range of the camp's golf course to the north and benefits from being oriented toward stunning mountain views to the south, looking toward the Northstar California Resort ski area—to which there is private direct ski access, as well as to parks, trails, and a nearby family barn. The surrounding tall pines prompted the clients to use wood as the primary building material and to match the lighter color of the tree bark. The designers selected clear cedar for that purpose and employed wood-burning techniques and staining to achieve an organic and genuine look. Cedar and natural sierra granite are used profusely. On the outside, they are accompanied by dark metal roofs, exposed blackened steel structural elements, stairs, and steel doors and windows. Timber posts are wrapped by hammered iron straps that add a medieval castle-like character to the house. The front door is made up of a blackened steel panel with a clear cedar accent strip and is marked by custom steel-clad lighting features over it. The front porch and broad gable roof over the great room in the back are both distinguished by expressive arched timber beams, the most charismatic and memorable exterior elements.

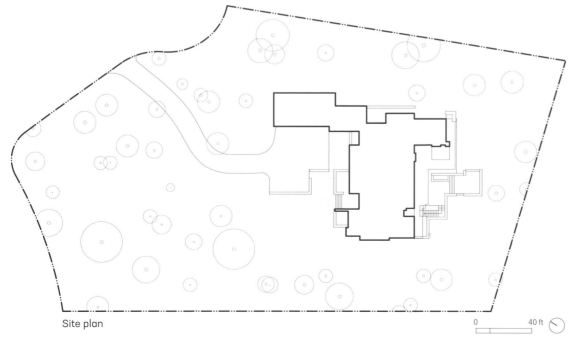

Site plan

0   40 ft

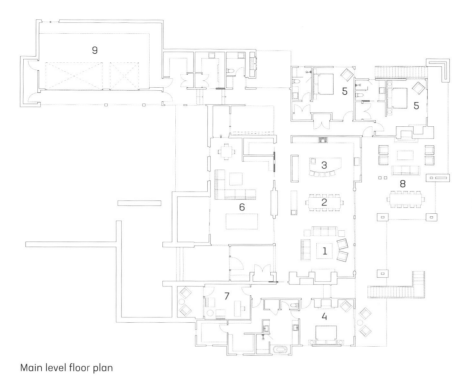

Main level floor plan

1 Great room
2 Dining
3 Kitchen
4 Master suite
5 Guest suite
6 Family room
7 Office
8 Terrace
9 Garage
10 Bunk room
11 Game room

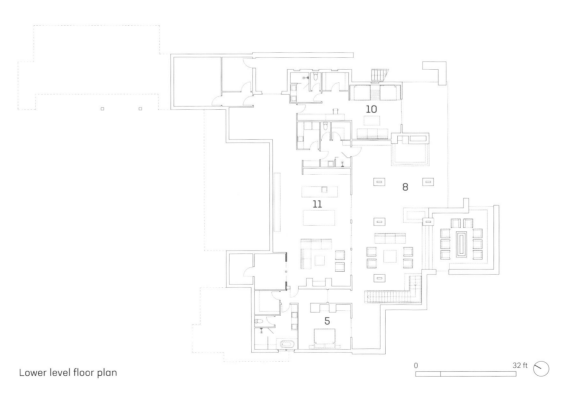

Lower level floor plan

0   32 ft

On the main level, apart from the three-car garage, which is attached through a mudroom in the east wing, the house is entered through a formal entry foyer that leads to a huge squarish space made up of a great room with a kitchen at its east end and a living room fireplace on the west side, and with auxiliary den, pantry, and a firepit patio next to the wet bar near the entry. The great room features a twenty-one-foot-high ceiling to the ridge and a system of curved and straight massive timber beams inscribed into two intersecting wood-clad gables. Other spaces on this level include a master bedroom to the west, and two guest suites to the east. There are three sets of stairs here—the interior stair in the east wing that connects to both the lower level and upstairs, and two exterior stairs. They conveniently link an extensive terrace that wraps the house on the southern side and includes outdoor living, dining, and firepit areas to the ground. The interior stair stands apart for its floating oak treads and the original baluster design—a lineup of closely spaced steel flat bars that form a continuous screen on the main floor—merges integrally with the handrail upstairs.

Downstairs has a large media room situated directly under the great room, another wet bar, wine storage, a guest suite, lots of storage spaces, and a huge bunker room for kids, providing the ideal setting to welcome a lot of people for entertainment. On the south side, the house is surrounded by interconnected patios, a large firepit with a custom stone-clad seating area, a spacious spa, patios for the guest bedroom suite and media room, and plenty of outdoor spaces. The topmost floor includes one additional and fully autonomous large guest bedroom suite with fireplaces and a compact deck facing north.

The interior, dominated by oak flooring, cedar structural members, and natural stone walls, feels and looks rich, warm, and rustic. The architects collaborated with Spearhead on such bespoke elements as timber structures, steel doorways and doors, and stair details. Other design features that add a special character to the house include authentic plaster walls, an iron stove hood in the kitchen, natural stone around the fireplace in the great room, custom concrete sinks, and lots of exposed steel details. They are skillfully combined with clean lines, sleek tiles and steel surfaces, refined cabinetry, and cool décor to balance between the traditional and more contemporary aesthetics of the husband and wife.

THUNDERBIRD COURT

Truckee, California, 2015

Thunderbird Court sits in close proximity to the public zone within Martis Camp luxury second-home community near Truckee, California. The house is a compact assemblage of familiar domestic forms, a handsome fusion of traditional sheltering roof gables hovering over massive stone walls and airy, contemporary volumes with extensive glazing, copper-clad pronounced bay windows with crisp glazed corners, and thick arched canopies, all "dancing" around two towering stone-clad chimneys. What makes this site quite special is its potential to capture the dramatic wooded landscape views all around, particularly the tip of the ski area to the northwest, which was one of the main intentions for acquiring this odd-shaped lot in the first place. The architect succeeded by aligning the great room's ridge perfectly with the mountaintop. This alignment is celebrated through oversized windows and clerestories, which bring lots of air and sunlight, and blur clear distinctions between inside and outside throughout. The house and site fit like a glove; it is nestled into the allowable building envelope so carefully that they come in contact in multiple spots. Other attractions for the owners—a family out of the San Francisco Bay area with three school children at the time when the house was built—include various community amenities virtually next door; most of all, a kids-centric family barn with a pond, entertainment, restaurant, and games.

In plan, the house is configured like a three-blade propeller with a two-car garage and attic above to the east, an outdoor living room—a covered patio with a fireplace—facing west, and a master suite at the southern end, all grouped around a courtly double-height great room at the core with adjacent kitchen and dining area. Two bedrooms upstairs—a bunk room and guest bedroom suite—are located above the outdoor living room and kitchen and dining area downstairs, while an intimate media room is situated right across from the stair with thick floating wood treads. An unusually large portion of this compact house is dedicated to the common areas. The great room is accessed through a formal foyer with a giant entry pivot door. It is eight feet wide and thirteen feet tall, a symbolic welcoming gesture to invite neighbors, many of whom have become friends of this family that enjoys entertaining guests and hosting parties.

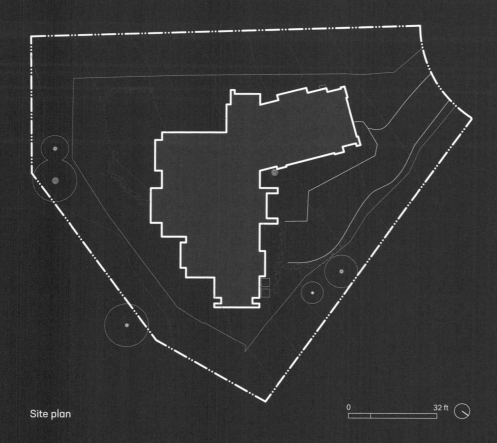

Site plan

0   32 ft

Throughout the house, both inside and out, three materials dominate—stone, wood, and glass. The stone—a sandstone ledge stone out of Montana is notable for its rigorous geometric pattern—a sequence of horizontal bands of several thicknesses to give this ancient material a contemporary character. Fortified low walls made of boulders, as well as loose boulders all around the house, bring a more-traditional feeling. Inside, full-height stone walls define the foyer, accent walls within the master bedroom suite and stair volume, and most prominently, the areas around the two oversized fireplaces—one in the great room and the other in the outdoor living room. One additional exterior material that turns the house into a handcrafted work of art is copper. Roofs are distinguished by handmade hammered copper shingles and patinaed copper panels wrap bay windows, several smaller volumes, and garage doors.

The juxtaposition of traditional and contemporary is the main theme of the design here. The façades feature wood siding, both laid out in a traditional horizontal pattern and accent areas arranged vertically in a contemporary manner. Within the house, walnut windows and cabinetry are complemented by European oak flooring, clear cedar ceilings in bedrooms, an outdoor living room, and a great room. The great room features castle-like oversized chandeliers, and the space's twenty-foot-tall cathedral ceiling is distinguished by curved trusses resting on two improbably long beams that run the entire length of the great room, puncturing the façades and projecting outwards at both ends. They are clad in Douglas fir timber but are actually made of steel, again, balancing playfully between the house's traditional materials and clean, contemporary geometry.

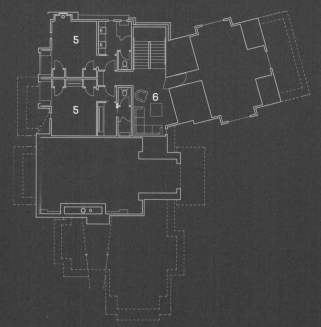

Upper level floor plan

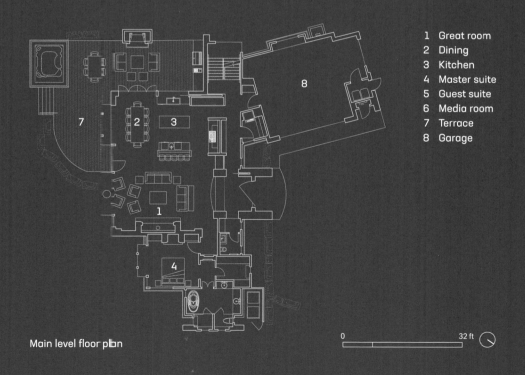

Main level floor plan

1 Great room
2 Dining
3 Kitchen
4 Master suite
5 Guest suite
6 Media room
7 Terrace
8 Garage

0   32 ft

ALMEDDRAL

Truckee, California, 2018

Situated in Martis Camp, south of Truckee, Almeddral is a mountain contemporary home that sits comfortably on a large 2.5-acre site, providing full privacy to its owners who split their time evenly between here and their home in the Bay area. The house is reached by a driveway, which is several hundred feet long, coming to a landscaped roundabout to the north of the main entrance, ennobling it with a sense of arrival. The house appears to be quite abstract and understated due to its clean laconic forms and disciplined use of just a few materials—vertical cedar siding, extensive glazing, and black-painted steel trims of flat and shed cantilevered roofs with cedar soffits. These dominating materials are accompanied by a few accent surfaces clad in painted light gray corrugated metal; one of them is an outdoor spa in the back, an apt hint of the industrial nature of some of the materials inside.

There are three main parts that comprise the house, each oriented in its own direction, effectively breaking its overall scale. The core assumes a rectangular volume along the east-west axis—a double-height great room with a kitchen and dining area, a guest bedroom suite linked through an enclosed bridge, and upstairs there are a couple of guest bedrooms, one of which is a bunk room, and a den/media room with a craft studio. Some of the bedrooms feature up to fourteen-foot ceilings lined in clear cedar. The two angled wings are single-level structures—the master bedroom suite with an office for the scientist-entrepreneur owner with a separate outdoor entry on the west end and a double-deep four-car garage at the opposite east end. The wings' angles are not quite parallel; they are defined by the site's grown trees and preferred views from within.

The house is oriented toward the southern mountain and ski area views in the back where the master suite and kitchen-dining area are extended deep into the wooded site to celebrate outdoor living and blur the line between inside and outside. The outdoor living space, accompanied by a broad stone-clad fireplace and kitchen through a sliding window, serves as a family-gathering space to enjoy summer sunsets. Extensive canopies are supported by a system of exposed steel columns, characteristically angled. Together with the steel beams that are elongated several feet into the air. They establish a dynamic rhythm and evoke a contemporary interpretation of brackets and knee braces of traditional Tahoe lodge wood-frame houses.

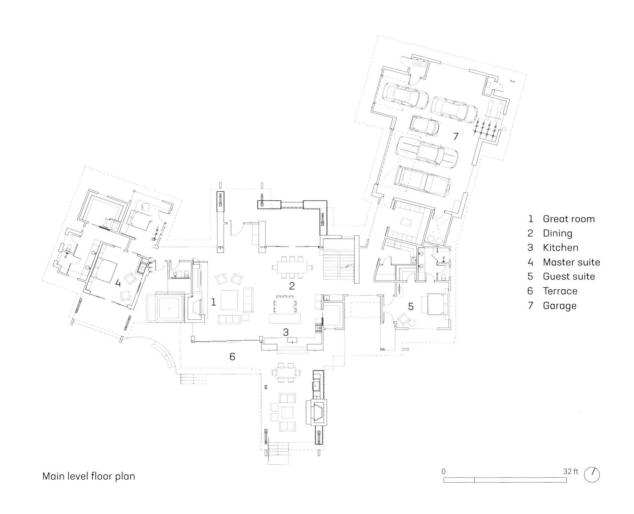

1 Great room
2 Dining
3 Kitchen
4 Master suite
5 Guest suite
6 Terrace
7 Garage

Main level floor plan

0   32 ft

The interior is a result of a collaboration between the architects and the interior designer, with whom Kelly|Stone Architects worked on several other houses in California and Hawaii. These spaces are distinguished by a strong holistic approach thanks most of all to the couple's shared design vision, which is rarely the case. The general direction here is expressed in contemporary minimalist sensibilities and juxtaposition of such contrasting materials as exposed steel beams, painted metal panels, clear cedar ceilings, walnut cabinets, and smooth drywall on the one hand with cut sandstone veneer walls in a brick-like pattern, hickory hardwood flooring, and nutty doorway trims on the other, achieving strong balance and a lot of character to otherwise clean spaces.

Just like in many other Kelly|Stone Architects-designed houses, the great room is locked between a hefty fireplace at one end and a custom kitchen range unit at the other; both are crafted of locally sourced granite. Another prominent anchor of this space is a connecting steel stair in the northeast corner. It is notable for its open risers and floating treads made of so-called parallel-strand lumber or Parallam, a synthetic timber, which is visually appealing and works well with the supporting steel structure. This large central space sits under a slanted ceiling that slopes up toward the south and peaks at eighteen feet where a massive glass wall opens under a clearstory to an expansive outdoor paved seating area punctuated with a firepit and fortified by decorative low walls made of boulders.

VILLANDRY CIRCLE

Truckee, California, 2017

Villandry Circle is one of several dozen houses that Kelly|Stone Architects designed in Martis Camp, a private ski and golf resort of a luxury second-home community near Truckee, California. There are nearly 650 homes here today with no more than one hundred lots remaining to be developed. Although, it is in all likelihood that most of those lots will stay vacant to preserve privacy and secure the existing sight lines for the current homeowners. The rigorously formed home sits in the center of its one-and-a-half-acre corner site on a gentle slope at a comfortable distance away from houses next door. A short driveway comes straight up from a slightly curving street to the east. It arrives at a compact auto court hugged by an L-shaped two-wing structure with east-facing views toward the ski areas hovering in the distance above the street.

The house stands out for its openness toward the densely forested lot on all sides and for being wrapped around by interconnected terraces and patios under sweeping shed roofs held by exposed steel columns—some standing straight up others leaning slightly outward. The first floor is sunk partially into the ground and framed by straight sections of board-form concrete walls that rise in steps as they follow higher elevation. These low-rise borders simultaneously provide more privacy and maximize views. Except for a few steps at the entrance and within the mudroom that links the house directly with the garage, the residential wing is conveniently situated on a single level. The garage is big enough to house a water ski boat, two cars, and a golf cart. The owner of the house, a San Francisco-based entrepreneur, and his young and active family spend at least half of their time here in Martis Camp to take advantage of the diverse outdoor lifestyle that it offers.

The southeast end of the residential wing is separated from the core of the dwelling—the great room, kitchen, and formal dining room behind sliding doors—by a bridge-like passage glazed on both sides. It leads to a large master suite that functions as a private apartment and features a master patio with a spa tub and a room-size closet expressed on the main façade as a prismatic volume clad in prefinished metal panels and cut with a clerestory window. Other ground-floor spaces include a bedroom-sized office—both for husband and wife—and an airconditioned gear room, adjacent to the garage. The latter is a giveaway of this young family and their kids' passion for an adventurist outdoor lifestyle, particularly focused on skiing—both snow and water—and mountain hikes. The enclosed stair behind the kitchen's pantry leads to the second floor that sits largely on top of the garage and comprises a junior master suite, guest suite, kids' bedroom with custom bunk beds, and media/recreation space, and culminates in a covered deck with a gas firepit along its edge with a sublime view of the mountain range toward the northeast.

Outdoor materials are mostly cedar siding, dry stack stone veneer, prefinished metal panel cladding, extensive glazing, exposed thin steel columns, and shed roofs with clear cedar undersides. The hardscape around the house, including planters made of board form concrete, was all designed by the architect. It is complemented by aspen trees and ornamental shrubs, all planted in close proximity to the house to soften the strong impact of native Jeffrey pines that dominate the landscape and enhance the indoor-outdoor connection.

The great room faces south toward the ski hill. Its ceiling reaches sixteen feet at the peak and through a large glazed wall, it transitions quite naturally into an extensive outdoor living area where sun exposure is maximized. Throughout the house, flat ceilings are plastered drywalls and all sloped ones are lined in clear cedar. Most of the exterior materials are brought inside—stone veneer walls give a strong character to the entry foyer and transition areas; they also define fireplaces. Exposed steel beams—vertical, horizontal, and angled—outline wide openings, support ceilings, and frame fireplaces in decorative but holistic gestures. Custom-cast architectural concrete panels are placed over fireplaces and make up the enclosure of the open riser steel stair with white oak threads, steel tube stringers, and steel-and-glass-guard rails with stainless-steel caps along glass edges. Handrails are made of steel square tubes to highlight the extensive use of exposed steel columns and beams, both inside and out. Floors throughout the house are dark-stained white oak and bathroom floors are finished in mosaic tiles. Cabinets are made of oak throughout the house to keep the material palette disciplined and to underline a sense of sleekness and continuity. Nooks and crannies in hallways provide cozy opportunities for such activities as playing cards and chess while constantly maintaining a strong connection to nature.

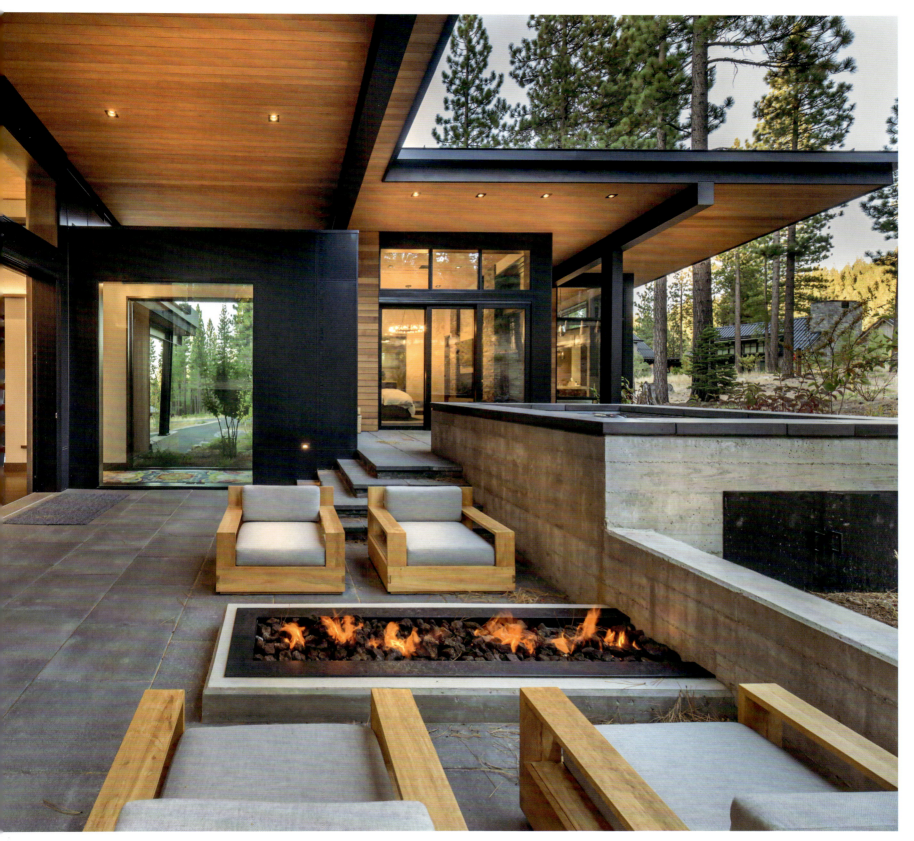

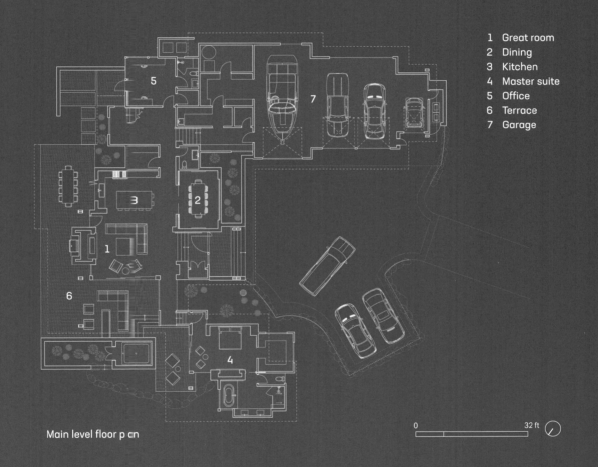

Main level floor p □n

1	Great room
2	Dining
3	Kitchen
4	Master suite
5	Office
6	Terrace
7	Garage

0   32 ft

EHRMAN DRIVE

Truckee, California, 2017

Ehrman Drive is a mountain contemporary vacation home built at Martis Camp community of luxury homes on the outskirts of Truckee, California. The house is situated on a down-sloping lot surrounded by tall pine trees with scarce vegetation and is pointing almost directly to the north toward elevated vistas of the Sierra Nevada and Carson ranges. The southern views that open from the front of the house face the Northstar California ski resort. This compactly planned structure was built on a relatively prudent budget when compared to other luxury private homes in this development. However, it was precisely the necessity to work with limited means that led to general simplicity, efficient plan and circulation, and rigorous planning and design decisions, which ultimately resulted in a very attractive structure; according to Kelly, one of his favorites. The house follows a clear L-shaped plan that hugs a rectangular auto court at the front. The driveway from across the plaza comes right between two large granite boulders.

The L's short leg to the east is a single-story three-car garage, while its long bar is a two-story dwelling stretched in the east-west direction—a single story on the uphill front side and two stories on the opposite downhill side in the rear. There is a clear visual hierarchy: the garage is a solid double volume topped by two roofs—a flat part over a single-car southern end and a shallow arch over a slightly higher double-car space. Higher still is a single-curved roof that sits comfortably over the main dwelling. It greets visitors with its largely glazed wide front. This generously gestured roof, easily the most prominent feature in the house, is punched through by a chimney behind and to the west of a minimalist central entry with a moderately scaled patio under a flat canopy. The exterior's front is clad in low-maintenance materials that combine quartz stacked stone veneer, board-formed concrete walls, rusted steel and prefinished metal panels, and cedar siding. The clerestory windows with understated mullions extending right to the bottom of the structure accentuate a sweeping curve of the roof that appears to be floating quite effortlessly.

The entry leads directly to an airy great room, which combines living, dining, and kitchen areas under a soaring twenty-foot ceiling with its characteristic long curved double glulam beams that fittingly sit on a pair of exposed steel cross beams. The massive timber beams effectively extend the length of the great room, while a wall of glass doors and clerestory windows dramatically expand outside views by bringing the surrounding pine treetops and daylight inside this seemingly boundless space.

The great room is anchored by a prominently designed fireplace on the west side. It is distinguished by the floor-to-ceiling backlit sculptural feature made of a single panel of Glass Fiber Reinforced Concrete (GFRC). It is framed by patinated steel panels and surrounded by a wall of white oak panels—some are touch latch doors to hide television and AV equipment and storage compartments behind to reinforce the clean modern aesthetic. The fireplace separates the great room from a stair volume directly behind it; this entire enclosure—windows, doors, treads, handrails, and cabinets are made from custom-designed rift-cut white oak panels. This abundance of light-colored wood matches hemlock curved timber beams, ceilings, and soffits, all characterized by very clean grain surfaces. The west end of the main level, which is right behind the stair, is reserved for the master bedroom suite; it is uniquely supported by a system of board form concrete walls, while a portion of the master bath is cantilevered over the site to the north.

The house belongs to a couple from Silicon Valley—he is a tech businessman and she is a painter; her art studio occupies a bedroom-size space on the opposite end of the dwelling, behind the L-shaped kitchen next to the garage. All spaces on the north side of this level are surrounded by generous terraces, projected over patios downstairs and supported by a series of exposed, thin, steel columns. The aforementioned stair volume is prominently defined on the northern façade by a tall window framed by rusted panels. The stair leads downstairs to the family media/playroom, bunk bedroom for two of the couple's kids, and two guest bedrooms. The playroom is separated from the stair by a full-height glass wall that supports the railing, and while it reduces the sound transmission, it maintains the visual connection on the lower level. All materials here are very durable, including large format porcelain tiles to wear well with kids, the environment, and the family's pets.

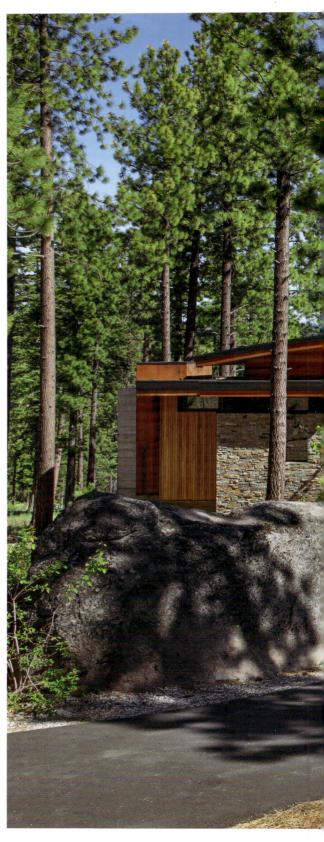

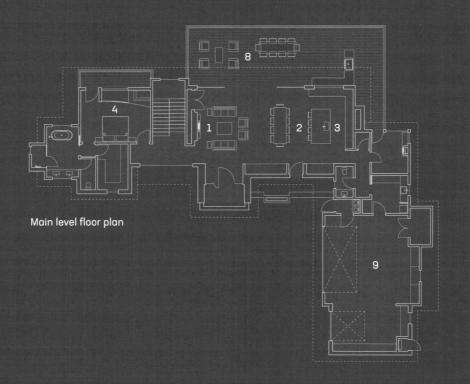

Main level floor plan

1 Great room
2 Dining
3 Kitchen
4 Master suite
5 Guest suite
6 Bunk suite
7 Media room
8 Terrace
9 Garage

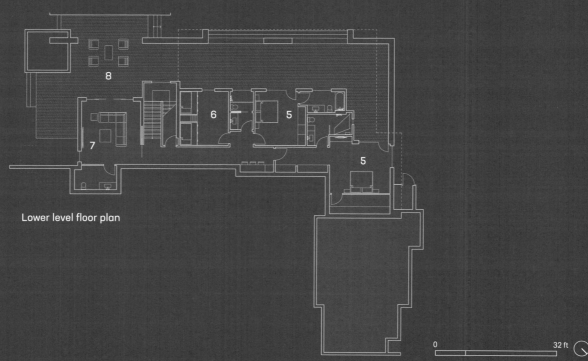

Lower level floor plan

0   32 ft

WYNTOON

Truckee, California, 2018

This secluded home is the second Martis Camp residence for its owners, originally from Michigan where they started Glenwood Mountain Homes, the construction company that built this house, and several other Kelly|Stone Architects-designed homes in this private luxury ski and golf community just south of Truckee, California. The owners, a couple with two grown children, used to vacation here and eventually decided to move to Martis Camp permanently, also living part-time in San Francisco. It was their encounter with several earlier houses designed by the architects that led to this collaboration. Recently, when the children left the family nest for college, the couple sold the house and moved to a smaller place in Nevada.

Wyntoon is set back from the road where it sits on a low-traffic cul-de-sac on a remote, one-acre site amid picturesque forest and mountain views, a unique spot, at a height of 6,000 feet, where no neighboring houses are visible in this almost 650-home community. The house follows an L-shaped plan where the living quarter's volume is stretched along an east-west axis and a large garage, set at 90 degrees to the living wing at the west end is designed to make it feel like an integral part of the main house, not a mere appendage. Both parts are similar in size and are topped by seemingly hovering shed roofs with clerestories, mimicking the scenic mountains that envelop the property from every direction. The living part of the house meets the driveway head-on; its central formal entry under a large, flat canopy splits the house's first floor into the master bedroom suite to the east and a great room-dining and kitchen area with a soaring eighteen-foot ceiling to the west. There are husband and wife offices behind the kitchen and garage; they can be converted into bedrooms with a shared bathroom in between.

The lower floor contains a gym, recreation/media room, and storage under the master bedroom suite on the main floor and two additional bedrooms under the behind-the-garage offices/bedrooms, bringing the total number of bedrooms to six. Transparency, natural daylighting, and passive solar design are the main design strategies here to take maximum advantage of this picturesque lot. It opens spectacularly on the back side with elevated unobstructed southern views of the valley between Martis Camp and the North Star Ski area. The house has direct access to the forest, which was the main reason for building such an unusually large garage for the family that enjoys outdoor living. This space is designed for at least three cars, several snowmobiles, motorcycles, mountain bikes, and other riding equipment. It also serves as an event space with a double-height ceiling and a bar. On the two-story southern side of the house, outdoor amenities include a firepit, a spa, and a patio, which leads directly to a network of nature trails extending through Tahoe National Forest.

The material and color palette—exposed concrete walls, dark corrugated metal siding, blackened steel panels, stone, vertical cedar accents, and extensive glazing—blend naturally with the site's gray boulders, soil, and pine needles. These durable materials limit exterior maintenance in the area's harsh climate. The poured concrete foundation supports a combination of steel and wood-frame structures with bulky exposed structural beams and columns. Interiors are enhanced by transitional views of distant mountain peaks and a dense pine forest, all rush in from every side, including in the most private areas such as bedrooms; some offer huge floor-to-ceiling glazed corners, equipped with solar shades. A deep sunken yard on the entry side before the great room allows plenty of daylight for the lower floor in addition to a generous glazing in the back on the south side. Throughout the house, the interiors feature large areas of blackened steel panels to underline the indoor-outdoor connection, lots of exposed steel structures, poured-in-place concrete walls, drywall, polished kitchen cabinets, and walnut floors. A floating steel-and-glass staircase and a dramatic fireplace framed by large W-flanges anchor opposite ends of the double-height great room topped by clerestories with the overpowering presence of the sky. The juxtaposition of rough and highly finished materials adds vividness to this hefty and seemingly unbound space.

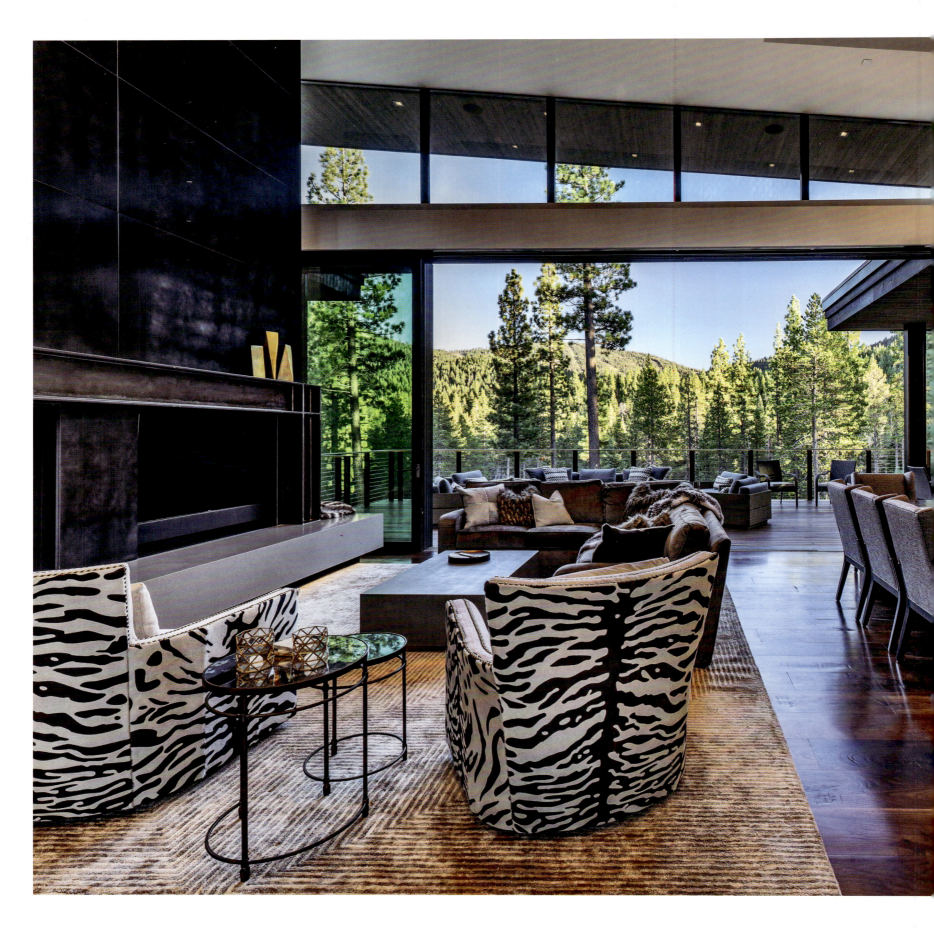

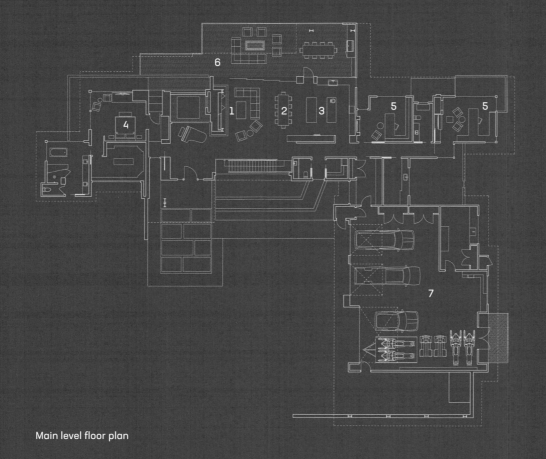

Main level floor plan

1 Great room
2 Dining
3 Kitchen
4 Master suite
5 Office
6 Terrace
7 Garage
8 Guest suite
9 Bunk room
10 Media room

Lower level floor plan

0   32 ft

NOHO KAI

Koloa, Kauai, Hawaii, 2021

Aptly nicknamed by its client, Noho Kai, which refers to a boy's name—the one who lives by the seashore—this house sits on a gorgeous cliff site overlooking the golf fairway, forty feet above the ocean, facing it head-on. It is the most critical advantage for picking this particular location: no other houses are visible from here toward the water. The property is part of Kukuiʻula, a resort community of luxury vacation homes in Koloa on the south shore of Kauai, the so-called "Garden Island" of the Hawaiian archipelago. The dynamically growing development sits on a former sugar plantation and, therefore, this home's appearance is rooted primarily in the design principles of traditional plantation houses, of course, enhanced by present-day requirements of comfortable and, no less critical, stylish living. The dwelling's owner who is based in Scottsdale, Arizona envisioned this house to be shared with his children and grandchildren. Now retired, he used to head the development company that was behind creating Kukuiʻula here on Kauai and Martin Camp in Truckee, California. Kelly|Stone Architects designed many of their homes in both developments.

The site is accessed via a narrow back road that parallels the shoreline and is shaped like an elongated parallelogram—about 100 feet wide and 270 feet long. There is a sequence of three main parts here—the house on a rectangular plot in the center; the arrival auto court on a trapezoidal area in front of it; and a trapezoid-shaped garden on the oceanfront side toward the southern end. This tip of the site evokes a feeling of being on a prow of a ship. The single-story house is made up of a nearly symmetrical group of pavilions lined up on either side of the great room in the center. A full-height stone wall with see-through cedar-slated gates separates the house from the auto court paved with lava stone inserted into a grass-planted geometric grid. A two-car garage is built as a pavilion extension to the house along the eastern edge of the site. The ocean-front area comprises a compact gas firepit surrounded by lush greenery with several solitary palm trees framing majestic ocean views.

The great room, a square in plan and, like the rest of the house, a timber structure, sits right on the central axis of the site. It is entered ceremoniously through a rectangular lanai fronted by a pair of low-rise stone walls. The great room's vast interior comprises dining and seating areas under a sixteen-foot-tall cathedral ceiling. The room opens fully by means of twenty-eight-foot wide by eleven-foot-tall sliding doors—the whole wall disappears and the interior opens on another lanai at least as big as the great room itself and followed by a forty-by-sixteen-foot infinity-edge pool with a corner spa. It effectively blends with the ocean and sky offering an uninterrupted and seemingly boundless oceanfront view. To the west of the great room lies a cluster of two master suites. The bigger one with the ocean view is reserved for the owners. The other one enjoys private interior garden views. These suites are separated by a bunk bedroom. On the opposite side to the east, behind the kitchen, there are two guest suites. Each of the four suites features its own garden with an outdoor shower surrounded by a full-height stone wall.

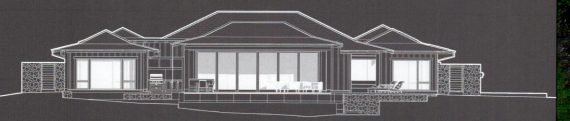

All spaces and windows situated at the southern end of the house are designed to capture and maximize impressive views toward the ocean and down the coast to accentuate a sense of perspective. Apart from the views, the interiors also celebrate intricately designed and built cathedral ceilings. Each pavilion has its own. The one in the great room is by far the largest and most remarkable. Designed and manufactured by Daizen Joinery timber frame professionals based out of Canada, it is characterized by a unique, self-supported, skeletal ceiling; it is made up of solidly built ridges and rafters and is held by a hidden steel frame. Painted white, this gorgeous structure contrasts vividly against the clear cedar underside of the actual roof above.

Exterior materials include puka lava stone site walls, painted reversed board and batten siding, horizontal wood slot siding, and cedar shake roofing. Interiors have teak floors throughout and mosaic and tile flooring in the bathrooms. There are marble walls in the kitchen and bathrooms. Lanai spaces that feature plenty of casual seating areas are paved in stone tile. Their placements, both in front of the house and behind it, enable residents to alternate them depending on the direction of the wind. All ceilings and beams are cedar. The main entry is distinguished by a four-inch-thick custom-designed teak door on four massive industrial hinges, a piece of art in its own right.

Main floor plan

1 Great room
2 Dining
3 Kitchen
4 Master suite
5 Jr master suite
6 Guest suite
7 Bunk suite
8 Garage
9 Pool

0   32 ft

Project Credits

FAIRWAY OVERLOOK (p18-35)

Design/Completion: 2013/2017

Location: Truckee, California

Site: 1 acre

Size: 6 bedrooms, 7,000 ft²

Architect: Keith Kelly

Interior Design: Martine Paquin Design

Builder: Mountain Craft Custom Homes

Stair Fabricator: Spearhead

Photography: Vance Fox Photography;
Cesar Rubio Photography

ANGLERS COURT (p36-45)

Design/Completion: 2016/2019

Location: Steamboat Springs, Colorado

Site: 2 acres

Size: 4 bedrooms, 4,500 ft²

Architect: Tim Stone, Jason Oldfather

Interior Design: Kelly|Stone Architects

Builder: CCH

Photography: Tim Stone; Dan Tullos, Mountain
Home Photography

HINMAN CREEK (p46-57)

Design/Completion: 2010/2012

Location: Clark, Colorado

Site: 70 acres

Size: Main residence, 4 bedrooms: 7,500 ft²,
Wine cave: 600 ft², Equestrian riding
arena: 14,000 ft², Barn: 3,600 ft²

Architect: Tim Stone

Interior Design: Kelly|Stone Architects

Builder: Dover Development and Construction

Timber Spearhead

Cabinetry/Casework Fedewa Custom Works

Photography: Tim Stone

PEARL STREET (p58-67)

Design/Completion: Two Stages: 2013/2014, 2015/2016

Location: Steamboat Springs, Colorado

Site: 7,000 ft²

Size: Home: 3 bedrooms, 1,950 ft²,
Accessory dwelling unit: 2 bedrooms, 650 ft²

Architect and Builder: Tim Stone

Interior Design: Kelly|Stone Architects

Subcontractors New Mountain Builders, Vaussa,
High Point Roofing

Photography: Tim Stone

NORTH ROUTT RETREAT (p68-75)
Design/Completion: 2010/2012
Location: Clark, Colorado
Site: 50 acres
Size: 4 bedrooms, 3,500 ft²
Architect: Tim Stone
Builder: Fox
Interior Design: Kelly|Stone Architects
Photography: Tim Stone; Dan Tullos, Mountain Home Photography

SWIFTS STATION (p76-85)
Design/Completion: 2017/2019
Location: Carson City, Nevada
Site: 2 acres
Size: 5 bedrooms, 7,000 ft²
Architect: Tim Stone
Builder: NSM
Interior Design: Kelly|Stone Architects
Photography: Paul Dyer Photography

BARN VILLAGE (p88-101)
Design/Completion: 2017/2020
Location: Steamboat Springs, Colorado
Site: ½ acre
Size: 4 bedrooms, 4,500 ft²
Architect: Tim Stone, Jason Oldfather
Builder: Shively Construct Inc.
Interior Design: Kelly|Stone Architects
Photography: Tim Stone; Dan Tullos, Mountain Home Photography

RADIUM HOT SPRINGS (p102-113)
Design/Completion: 2012/2014
Location: Radium Hot Springs, British Columbia, Canada
Site: 50 acres
Size: 6 bedrooms, 3,500 ft²
Architect: Tim Stone
Rammed Earth Sidewall
Timber Spearhead
Interior Design: Kelly|Stone Architects
Photography: Tim Stone

KAHALAWAI (p114-23)
Design/Completion: 2014/2017
Location: Koloa, Hawaii
Site: 68 acres
Size: 6 bedrooms, 7,000 ft², including outdoor space
Architect: Keith Kelly
Builder: Greenwood
Landscape Architect: Greg Boyer
Interior Design: Kelly|Stone Architects
Photography: Gregory Blore, Alohaphotodesign

COPELAND LANE (p124-31)
Design/Completion: 2007/2012
Location: Truckee, California
Site: 1.2 acres
Size: 6 bedrooms, 8,400 ft²
Architect: Keith Kelly, Tim Stone
Builder: Greenwood Homes
Interior Design: American Artisans
Photography: Tim Stone; Joy Strotz, Strotz Photography

CARSON VISTA (p132-41)

Design/Completion: 2014/2017
Location: Truckee, California
Site: 2 acres
Size: 6 bedrooms, 8,230 ft²
Architect: Keith Kelly
Builder: Colby Mountain Properties
Interior Design: Kelly|Stone Architects
Photography: Paul Hamill Photography

HALE ʻO LUNA O KA LĀLA (p142-53)

Design/Completion: 2016/2018
Location: Kauai, Hawaii
Site: 1 acre
Size: 4 bedroom suites, 5,500 ft²
Architect: Keith Kelly
Builder: Greenwood Homes
Interior Design: Keith Kelly
Photography: Gregory Blore, Alohaphotodesign

E KOMO MAI (p154-65)

Design/Completion: 2015, 2018/2022
Location: Koloa, Hawaii
Site: 1 acre
Size: 4 bedrooms and office, 4,360 ft²
Architect: Keith Kelly
Builder: Glenwood Mountain Homes
Interior Design: Keith Kelly
Photography: Gregory Blore, Alohaphotodesign

KINGSCOTE COURT (p166-79)

Design/Completion: 2017/2019
Location: Truckee, California
Site: 1.6 acres
Size: 6 bedrooms, 9,000 ft²
Architect: Keith Kelly
Builder: Jim Morrison Construction
Interior Design: KTG Design
Photography: Nick Sorrentino, Photographer

THUNDERBIRD COURT (p180-91)

Design/Completion: 2012/2015
Location: Truckee, California
Site: ⅓ acre
Size: 3 bedrooms, 3,200 ft²
Architect: Keith Kelly
Builder: Laborde Builders
Interior Design: Kelly|Stone Architects and owners
Photography: Vance Fox Photography

ALMEDDRAL (p192-203)

Design/Completion: 2015/2018
Location: Truckee, California
Site: 2.5 acres
Size: 4 bedrooms and craft studio, 5,000 ft²
Architect: Keith Kelly
Builder: Glenwood Mountain Homes
Interior Design: Ryan Group Architects
Photography: Roger Wade Studio Inc.

VILLANDRY CIRCLE (p204–215)

Design/Completion: 2016/2017
Location: Truckee, California
Size: 4 bedrooms, 5,000 ft²
Site: 1.5 acres
Architect: Keith Kelly
Builder: Jim Morrison Construction
Interior Design: Kelly|Stone Architects
Photography: Vance Fox Photography

EHRMAN DRIVE (p216–27)

Design/Completion: 2014/2017
Location: Truckee, California
Site: 1 acre
Size: 4 bedrooms, Art studio, 5,150 ft²
Architect: Keith Kelly
Builder: Glenwood Mountain Homes
Interior Design: Kelly|Stone Architects
Photography: Roger Wade Studio Inc.

WYNTOON (p228–37)

Design/Completion: 2015/2018
Location: Truckee, California
Site: 1 acre
Size: 6 bedrooms, House: 6,300 ft².
  Garage: 2,000 ft²
Architect: Keith Kelly
Builder: Glenwood Mountain Homes
Interior Design: Ryan Group Architects
Photography: Paul Hamill Photography

NOHO KAI (p238–51)

Design/Completion: 2017/2021
Location: Koloa, Kauai, Hawaii
Site: 73 acres
Size: 5 bedrooms, 6,000 ft²
Architect: Keith Kelly
Builder: Pac Build
Interior Design: Vallone
Photography: Gregory Blore, Alohaphotodesign

Special Thanks

Kelly|Stone Architects extends a special thanks to the Book Production Team: Tim Stone, Keith Kelly, Naser Elayyan, Eleazar Quintanilla, Sarah Fisher, and Mahdi Elayyan. Our grateful thanks also to Viviana Aguilar Torres at Morpho Studio, Costa Rica.

Published in Australia in 2024 by
The Images Publishing Group Pty Ltd
ABN 89 059 734 431

Offices

Melbourne
Waterman Business Centre
Suite 64, Level 2 UL40
1341 Dandenong Road
Chadstone, VIC 3148
Australia
Tel: +61 3 8564 8122

New York
6 West 18th Street 4B
New York, NY 10011
United States
Tel: +1 212 645 1111

Shanghai
6F, Building C, 838 Guangji Road
Hongkou District, Shanghai 200434
China
Tel: +86 021 31260822

books@imagespublishing.com
www.imagespublishing.com

A catalogue record for this
book is available from the
National Library of Australia

Title: Mountain to Coast: Kelly|Stone Architects 20 Houses
Author: Edited by Vladimir Belogolovsky, Foreword by Peter Morris Dixon
ISBN: 9781864709483

This title was commissioned in IMAGES' Melbourne office and produced as follows: *Editorial* Danielle
Hampshire, Jeanette Wall, *Graphic design* Ryan Marshall,
Art direction/production Nicole Boehringer, *Senior editorial* Gina Tsarouhas

Printed on 140gsm Da Dong Woodfree paper (FSC®) in China by Artron Art Group

IMAGES has included on its website a page for special notices in relation to this and its other
publications. Please visit www.imagespublishing.com